Snowbird Stories:

Several Degrees beyond Common Sense

and
Some Poetry

A Memoir
Tjaakje C. Heidema

"Snowbird Stories: Several Degrees beyond Common Sense," by Tjaakje C. Heidema. ISBN 978-1-60264-799-2.(Softcover) . ISBN 978-1-60264-798-5 (Ebook).

Published 2011 by Virtualbookworm.com Publishing Inc., P.O. Box 9949, College Station, TX 77842, US. ©2011, Tjaakje C. Heidema. All rights reserved. No part of this publication may be reproduced, stored in a retrieval system, or transmitted in any form or by any means, electronic, mechanical, recording or otherwise, without the prior written permission of Tjaakje C. Heidema.

Manufactured in the United States of America.

Snowbird Stories:

Several Degrees beyond Common Sense

and Some Poetry

By the same author

Sweeping Away the Sand

This is a memoir. The names, places and events were real. The thoughts, behaviors and actions of the people as described, however, are the end product of the author's perception, memory and imagination. Therefore, parts of it may well be fiction.

The photo of the trumpeter swan on the cover was taken from a larger photograph by Ron Southworth entitled "Flight." It has been reprinted with his permission.

This book is dedicated to

Sophia

whose loyalty sustains
whose light brightens
whose humor lifts
and
whose love heals

Acknowledgements

I give a big thank you to all the neighbors and people who have filled and continue to fill my life with humor, lessons and stories.

Sophia, my life partner, I thank you so very much for being funny, generous and a good sport. Writing, preserving and publishing the stories has been possible because of your unwavering support and encouragement.

Thank you, Louise, for helping to move my project forward with the initial proofing and for always being supportive of my journey. The bulk of the proofreading and editing was done by Vangi De Master. A talented teacher, Vangi educated, illumined, supported and nudged me along with her comments. Thank you, Vangi, for adding sophistication and companionship to my efforts.

Table of Contents

Stories from Maine   1

   Several Degrees beyond Common Sense   2

   An Irregular Irregularity   10

   "Damned Liar of a Doctor"   18

   Tragedies, Talents and Tangles   24

And Stories from Arizona   37

   In Desperate Need of a Guardian   38

   That Old, Old Story   45

   The Art of Small Talk   51

   Will the Real April Fool Please Stand Up   56

From Maine Again   63

   In-Laws: Ya Gotta Love Em!   64

   A Swift, Sharp Verbal Blow   77

   Some New Wrinkles in the Routine   83

   Mrs. Firth Lies in Repose   87

And from Arizona Again   101

   I'm a Junky and I Have Mrs. Simon Cole to Blame   102

   People Who Live with Pets Do Better   112

   The Farewell Luncheon Debacle   126

   End of Life Issues   137

Some Poetry   155

Stories from Maine

Chapter One

Several Degrees beyond Common Sense

I AM A WOMAN, and as such I am quite comfortable with the fact that many years ago I let my biological clock tick down to complete silence without ever having given birth to a baby. I have also, I might add, never been a mother to a baby—not adopted, test tube, surrogate or any other way. Believe it or not, I have never wanted to have a baby or ever dreamt of having one.

Sure, as a teenager I did baby-sit, which naturally included infants sometimes, but that activity of mine was motivated not by any maternal instincts but by my yearning to have that new, green Schwinn bicycle with the narrow tires from Sears and Roebuck. And, too, as a student nurse in a three-year diploma program in my twenties, I did a three-week mandatory block of time on the maternity floor. Those days, though, were more than 25 years ago when huge rooms were still referred to as wards and when there could be as many as twenty women in one—ancient history, in other words.

This is what I remember of that experience: a seasoned mother, who was very pretty with thick, long, auburn-colored hair—I can still see her so clearly in my mind's eye—was surprised and pleased when a second baby, a twin, slipped out of her right after the first. This was in pre-sonogram days; the doctor had not heard a second heartbeat nor suspected anything from the size of her abdomen; there had been no forewarning. And she was so cool with it! I remember nothing about either baby but I remember her reaction.

Snowbird Stories: Several Degrees Beyond Common Sense

In the intervening years, I have timidly set foot on a birthing unit only once. It had nothing to do with me; I went to visit Elinor, my good friend. She'd had her baby.

So, to underscore, I have no personal or professional experience in obstetrics (O.B.) maternity, birthing, prenatal or nursery. Not even in gynecological. Yet, there I was, a school of nursing faculty member, assigned to O.B. as a clinical instructor for the entire fall semester! It was unconscionable, unchangeable and I am doomed.

This miserable fate of mine is the result of the University of Southern Maine School of Nursing in Portland having what is called an "integrated curriculum" approach. As explained to me—via the telephone during my long distance job interview while I was lounging in my bathrobe on the couch in my condominium in Denver—this approach entails the ability of teachers to be flexible. No kidding! Hypothetically, they had said, a psychiatric nurse specialist like you would be expected to handle and teach the normal psychological aspects of pregnancy. Yes, I could, I had decided after a bit of hesitation during the call; I could equate pregnancy to other adjustment situations in life, like divorce and death. Adjustment to change is always a challenge and any disorder in adjustment must be similar, I had brilliantly surmised. Pregnancy complicated by an already existing mental illness or even a postpartum depression with its delusions and hallucinations didn't scare me away either; I could handle those. But now! Now it is the boggy uterus, the episiotomy care, and the infant refusing the nipples that worry me. What do I know of these things? Nothing, nada, cero!

Synonyms for *flexible* in my big American Heritage Dictionary include *elastic, resilient, springy* and *supple*. Flexible I do; but contorting—*to bend, wrench or twist severely out of shape*—I do not. Not well anyway. Aw geez, I am so screwed.

Wreathed in this miasma of fear and impending disrepute, I went to my first meeting on the maternity unit in Weber Hospital today. The hospital, I had learned, was located in the town of Biddeford, midway between Portland and my home in Wells. Claire and Phyllis, two gray-headed old gals who are veteran O.B. nurses and long-time tenured faculty members, had set up the meeting as they had to reacquaint themselves with the staff and to orient me to the unit. Each, I had been informed, would have their own groups of students at the hospital on days I did not.

I arrived on time wearing street clothes, praying it would be an easy hour or two of touring and talking without the pressure or need to perform. If so, no problema. This was late summer prep work for faculty; students have not yet started the school year. I was already thinking ahead to when I would zip back home and take an inspiring walk on the beach.

In the hospital lobby we had hardly exchanged pleasantries before Phyllis and Claire turned on their heels—both, I noticed, were wearing white nurses' shoes—and walked me to the bank of elevators. Claire pushed the button for third floor and Phyllis, with her back to me, commenced gossiping with Claire about school politics. *So*, I grumbled internally, *this is how it is going to be.*

Did I mention that they were longtime faculty members? That I am untenured and thus lower in the pecking order? Or that they are maternity and I am psychiatric? Whatever. Who can stand this cliquish stuff, this cat fighting if that's what it is? My experience has been in the psychiatric clinical setting in a state hospital. There we mingled with lots of male staff. In my opinion, the guys made a huge positive difference. We had Friday afternoon clubs and danced on restaurant tables. We had affairs, even marriages, but cliques? Not so much.

Arriving on the third floor we three—Phyllis and Claire walking shoulder to shoulder, me behind—passed tightly wrapped bundles of flannel in plastic bassinets behind picture windows and entered a room labeled "Lounge." Phyllis and Claire each took a large white scrub dress from a stack on a table and proceeded on to an adjoining locker room. The ladies are quite stout, to put it mildly, and being six feet one inch tall and lean, I chose a medium size and followed.

The two, oblivious to my presence, stripped down to their white lacey slips and put on their dresses. They were talking nonstop, a whole summer's worth of stuff, you understand. I removed my belted brown and black over blouse, took off my black open-toed sling-backed patent leather pumps and removed my black slacks. Then I put my pumps back on and pulled the dress over my head. Unperturbed, I watched the hem of the dress settle six to eight inches above my knees. It was right after that split second of serenely watching the dress settle that my brain recognized the potential for me becoming an object of ridicule. Adrenaline and horror coursed through my body. Twelve to fifteen inches separated the bottom of the white dress from the top of my black knee-high stockings! Between the two were my bare-skinned, large-boned, pale, inward-tending knees with blonde hairs sticking up!

It had never occurred to me that I would have to disrobe and wear a dress. We never wore uniforms of any kind in psychiatry and, in general, I don't wear dresses anymore. The pantyhose were never long enough for my long legs and the crotch would always work its way downward with every step I took. I hated that.

Claire and Phyllis looked smug in their large dresses, and my first desperate attempt to save face was to quickly change from a medium to an extra-large size dress in hopes that the extra width would contribute some to the length. Only an inch or two at most were subtracted from the gap.

Being three times trained not to react—first as an immigrant who tried to pass as a citizen, then as an overly-tall woman who was stared at a lot, and finally as a psychiatric professional who was familiar with taking in shocking material as if she were a blank screen—I held my panic in check. I was at a loss but, by gum, these two O.B. plump-olas were not going to see me sweat.

Feigning good humor, I said "Ladies, I realize being integrated is an expectation of the job, and I will adjust, but this is ridiculous! Can you help me out here? Any suggestions?"

When people pass from common sense to intellectual pursuits, they are given degrees and these two colleagues of mine had advanced several degrees beyond common sense. They briefly glanced up but, not even seeing my dilemma, they ignored my spluttering and prattled on ad nauseum about issues between the faculty and the dean. What side was Paula, Dean Coneley's close associate, really on? Like it mattered!

Self-esteem draining away, I could think of not a single solution. I began to feel like a poor distant cousin of Big Bird—colorless, with the exception of my black feet and ankles, unheralded and defeated despite good intentions. Human unprofessional tears gathered in my eyes. *Great*, I thought self-deprecatingly, *another reason to be embarrassed*.

It didn't help, I knew, that I had found this lump in my breast more than a month before and that I was ashamed at the size of it and that I was having to wait to have it removed because I was on antibiotics for a lingering upper respiratory infection and that I was worried half to death about it being cancerous and that it might metastasize during the wait and that I couldn't share any of this with these two old laying hens because they didn't know or care about me.

I discovered the "swollen area"—that is what I wrote in my journal, I couldn't even call it a lump at first—on Sunday, July 26th, 1987; I had just turned 44. It was so humid and hot that day. Sophia, my partner, was involved in a family reunion over at her brother's house and I was in the shower getting ready to go over, too. My hand sought out this marble-sized lump in my right breast before I even realized there was soreness in the area. And the nipple was slightly retracted! Waves of fear and shame washed over me. *How could it have grown so big without me feeling it?* Finally, I rationalized that it probably was just an area of mastitis caused by a spider bite; I had trimmed bushes the week before. I had also been having an elevated temperature for a few days and what I had thought was a flu virus quite likely wasn't. It was all due to an infection in my breast.

The passage of time without resolution of the lump corrected my faulty reasoning, but it wasn't until August 17th that I could get in to have a mammogram. After that, I had a short delay until I could get a sonogram and still another week went by before I could see my gynecologist. When she did the exam, she was grim about my "hardened mass" and personally walked me over to a surgeon's office. He did a needle biopsy that same day.

Unlike the gynecologist, the surgeon was encouraging; he assured me that my history, the x-rays and his exam did not automatically lead him to a conclusion of cancer. I elaborated on my history—a paternal aunt and her daughter have both had mastectomies; this cousin has also had a recurrence of the breast cancer in her bones—but he remained hopeful. It could be an inflammatory process, he said, and I wanted to believe him. I wanted to slip back into my initial denial but I no longer could. I had come too far; I had, in fact, dreamt quite vividly the night before that it was cancer.

When I saw him again this past Friday, September 5th, he, too, was singing a different tune. Biopsies of my breast and underarm lymph nodes under general anesthesia are indicated, he had said and added: "This will include a frozen section and possible mastectomy if cancerous."

Two weeks of antibiotics for any lingering respiratory infection that I may have will take us to mid-September. Then, surgery is scheduled for the end of the month. My compromised respiratory status is bound to be a factor, not just for surgery but for any further treatment if indicated, and that's worrisome.

As I stood transfixed in the lounge of the maternity unit and as the tears threatened to overflow onto my white dress, a goddess—I swear she was—tapped me gently on my arm. She leaned in and whispered, "Psssst. I think this might help."

An inconspicuous—yet acutely aware and sensitive—hospital maid had witnessed the unfolding melodrama and had procured a white scrub pants from the doctors' lounge. Bless her heart! This dear woman was unafraid to care for me, a stranger.

On a daily basis, people like her keep me and all of us humans glued together, don't they? They just seem to have an intuitive sense of what is needed in certain circumstances and are not the least bit afraid to interject what it is they have to offer. Sometimes it is nothing more than a look directly into someone's eyes and a warm smile but, wow, can those make a difference! The spontaneous gifts of such folks reassure all of us that caring, compassion, joy and love really do exist.

I wanted to hug my benefactress, to tell her that she had just made a huge difference in my life and I would consider it an honor if she would have me for a friend. Instead, I uttered multiple words of gratitude and quickly slipped the pants on underneath my dress. I had to hurry to find my compatriots; they had headed out the door without as much as a backward glance.

While being introduced to white clad staff everywhere, I was still acutely self-conscious of my black feet and ankles, but oh so grateful, it wasn't what might have been. Grateful too, that my despair about life's injustices had been quelled by the kindness of a good soul.

May I be graced with more such benevolence in the weeks to come as I face my upcoming surgery and teach students, in the meanwhile, to assess post-partum bleeding by counting the number of sanitary pads a mother uses and by palpating flaccid abdomens to determine the firmness of uterine fundi. I will be stroking tiny cheeks of newborns so the students can see that the strokes encourage infants to root for dripping nipples. Did I really mean to say root? Probably not. That sounds more like something a farm animal would do. There must be another word these maternity people use for that.

Chapter Two

An Irregular Irregularity

As a student of nursing, I was taught to describe the many and varied rhythms of the human heartbeat. There is the straight forward staccato, the lub-dub of a dripping faucet, the pounding hooves of wild horses and, if lucky, one will feel and/or hear the much romanticized stop of the heartbeat for a second or two. There may be a flutter and a thud, even a plod or a wisp.

These rhythms, from my experience, can reach orchestrated complexity. For instance, a pause may be followed by a thud, both of which may occur once in four beats, and then the pattern repeats. One must carefully chart not only the type(s) of rhythm(s) but also, according to Mrs. Brooks, my Nursing Arts instructor of long ago, whether it is a regular irregularity or an irregular irregularity.

This intriguing terminology for rhythms came to mind when I was thinking about how best to describe my assigned nurse, Fran. It is October the third and I am not on the maternity unit as an instructor at Weber Hospital because I have had to undergo a mastectomy and am a patient, instead, in York Hospital in York, Maine. Right now, I am somewhere between hallucinating from my morphine drip and being discharged. A couple of days ago I was considered a "partial"—somewhere between a complete bath in bed and self care. I was a "partial" and Fran—clearly over fifty though she dyes her hair to appear younger—is part-time, I am no longer assigned to Fran but we bonded somehow and she still comes to see me.

Fran's nature falls within the irregular irregular variety. Her mind jerk-starts, ambles and races. When she took care of me lots of things moved about in a slow-motion frenzy and often ended up right where they started. To me there was no discernible synchronization between verbal expression and behavior. For instance, having pumped up the blood pressure cuff on my arm to an uncomfortable tight squeeze, but before she put the stethoscope in her ears, she bemoaned the fact that she had forgotten to take something out of the freezer and that her husband certainly could not be relied upon to do so and that maybe she could add the peas to the macaroni and cheese instead of the salad.

The notable exception in this non-pattern, pattern was Fran's mood. Despite unlimited spills, mistakes, all sorts of awkwardisms and annoyances, Fran wore a pleasant and kind expression. It seemed that within her was this stiff determination to present an unflappable temperament to the world.

"I don't want to complain, but I thought you would appreciate my suggestion..." Fran remarked pleasantly, when she was assigned an add-on patient in mid-morning. It was a tough add-on;

Mrs. B., was a "complete." The only clue to a less than pleasant underlying feeling in Fran, from my observation, was a slight droop of one of her eyelids. The curve of her mouth, I noticed, stayed stuck in a slight smile. In fact, Fran's face is disquietingly similar to the face of a panda bear. It is round, without wrinkle or angle and holds an expression of innocence untouched by the hands of time.

At the outset of my "partial", at 9:30 a.m., subliminally anticipating problems perhaps, I had explained briefly the previous day's routine to Fran. It had all gone so very well: I had been assigned to a neat, trim, mid-forty-ish bank manager-turned-nurses' aide "for a change" according to her. She had efficiently put a basin with warm sudsy water on a straight-backed chair in the small bathroom; I had sat on the towel-draped toilet stool lid and with the use of my left hand and arm—it is fortunate that I am left-handed, since my right arm is still in a sling. Too much movement of my right arm and shoulder, they said, could disturb the skin flaps or the drains coming out of the incision—leisurely soaked and dried my face, right arm, abdomen and thighs, ended my efforts by easing the basin onto the floor and soaked my feet. The privacy of those moments had been pure bliss after having been a "complete" for a couple days.

Ms. Bank V.P. had come in, changed the water and washed my itchy back. She had dried and powdered it carefully and then had left me to run the soothing water efficiently onto my pubis, into the toilet. So, at ten a.m., having been cleansed, dried and powdered all within no more than a half-hour, I had sat in my fresh gown in my fresh bed, soothed and relaxed. I had read a few cards, made the selections on the next day's menu, chatted with the maid, written in my journal and had felt fully prepared to graduate to self-care. I had actually had the thought that life would be all right again, thanks in no small part to Ms. Bank V.P.

However, this was not Ms. Bank V.P.; this was Fran. She wildly whipped off my top sheet and related that her sister had breast cancer and was still alive after four operations. I digested that startling tidbit as I swung my legs over the side of the bed and watched Fran pick up the straight-back chair. Then she set it back down and reflected aloud on sister's series of ever newly appearing tumors. As she did so, the drinking glass was moved from the over-bed table to the bedside stand, the water pitcher was refilled with ice water and the basin was pulled from under the stand and placed on the over-bed table.

"She has no breasts now and the cancer has probably spread to her bones," announced Fran as she watered the flowers. "Oh," she exclaimed, "I forgot to bring the linens. I'll be right back."

After a few minutes I swung my legs back up onto the bed, covered up best I could and surreptitiously examined my remaining breast for lumps. As I groped about, I became aware for the first time of the hollowness on my right side. My right breast was totally gone! The realization saddened me deeply. I would like to have washed it clean of the blood, put it into a satin-lined box and given it a nice burial, I reflected gloomily. Instead, it is alone, maybe on a warehouse shelf in an already forgotten jar of formaldehyde or already strewn about in the form of ashes in a landfill. What right did they have to keep it?

A half-hour or more crept by before Fran returned with the linen. She placed it in the easy chair across the room and launched into her opinion on the oncologist in residence at the hospital.

"He's okay, very technical. No bedside manner. His nurse either. She used to work here and left under suspicious circumstances. Don't ask me what; I don't know. She should have been let go instead of transferred in my opinion. No people skills."

The water glass came back to the over-bed table; the linen moved from the chair to the bed and the pillowcase was taken off my pillow. At 10:30, when an hour had elapsed with no progress on my "partial," Fran was called out to attend to Mrs. B.

Ninety-four year-old Mrs. B., I knew, had tried to die two nights earlier but she had been downright unlucky; the nurse had caught her at it. The public address voice at 3:45 a.m. had repeated three times: Cardiac Conference in Room 116—like any of us conscious patients believed that at that hour—Cardiac Conference in Room 116, Cardiac Conference in Room 116! It had been delivered in a studied monotone and provided background cadence for the many hurried footsteps going by my room in the hallway. One pair of feet had come back slowly and I heard a voice say to the desk clerk, "There are a hundred people in there."

Later I learned that Mrs. B's son was out-of-state, as was her niece. They are her only remaining relatives and neither of them has told the doctor to write the "No Code" order for her. Therefore, Mrs. B. was alive and not at all well. Lois, a friend who is a gerontologist, visited with me yesterday and, as we listened to Mrs. B.'s almost constant wails of, "Noooooo" or "Hellllllp", we chatted about the error someone had made. Clearly, we concurred, Mrs. B. should have been a slow code; they should have dragged their feet, in other words.

After Lois left, I had this urge to slip into Mrs. B's room, lock the door behind me and say, "Now! You have time. The door is locked. Go now, I'll stand watch. Quickly, slip away and do not look back." I don't think of pulling a plug or injecting a drug or anything; I just want to give permission as one human to another.

But, I digress.

So it was past 11:00 a.m. when Fran and I finally made it into the bathroom. Instead of one chair she had managed to place two straight-backed chairs in the small space. One was in front of the sink facing away from the sink and the other was in front of the toilet. That one had a basin of water on it with a washcloth in the water.

Fran instructed me to sit on the one with my back to the sink. This I did. As I reached across my body with my left hand for the washcloth in the cooled water, I became aware that Fran had quite a different plan in mind. She was squeezing between my right knee, the second chair and the toilet and standing at the sink by my right shoulder. From there she reached for the basin and refilled it with warm the water from the sink. Then she instructed me to wash my face which I did. Upon finishing, Fran untied my gown, took up the washcloth and scrubbed what she could of my front with my gown falling in a dejected heap at my feet. Sitting stark naked, I recall making some feeble stabs at introducing logic and expediency, but all to no avail. Fran had launched into more of her musings.

"Buy your wig before you start chemotherapy," she advised. "Don't wait until you're holding a clump of hair in your hand! Order your prosthesis, too, and make sure it is the right size. My sister..."

Fran changed the water again and, holding the basin aloft, squeezed her way back out so that she stood facing me. As it was told of a woman in the Bible who washed the feet of Jesus, Fran did likewise. She bent down and placed the basin at my feet then sank down onto her knees on my gown with her white shoes and white nylons extending out the bathroom door! She washed and dried my legs and feet—chattering the whole time—raised up her torso and reached over the back of me and my chair. I leaned to my left as she stretched and pressed her breast into my tender hollow side. Pressure on the drain caused a sudden sharp pain and I leaned further to the left to give her more room. It was her intent to dislodge the powder on the ledge above the sink. Barely able to jostle the powder with her fingertips, it toppled off the ledge, careened against the side of the sink and bounced beyond me into the basin of water on the floor. Reflexively, I tried to reach out to help but pulled back with a moan.

"...and for God's sake don't go to the oncologist by yourself, especially not the first time," instructed Fran unfazed by circumstances. "Call me. Call me anytime..."

Not once did Fran break her irregular, irregular rhythm in her version of my "partial." We were like the comedy team of Laurel and Hardy. Those two were often hopelessly entangled in one of their adventures gone bad and, like them, Fran and I plunged on to conclusion.

"My sister is still so angry she won't go to any support group meetings but I go and I'm learning many tips," said Fran as she put my fresh gown on backwards and almost stepped in the basin still setting on the floor. Water sloshed around in the basin and out onto the floor. She laid down a towel, took my hand and maneuvered me past the basin; then she bent down to mop the floor with the abandoned gown.

At last I sat in a chair near my bed, toyed with the cold lunch food, and waited for Fran to change the sheets and restore the bathroom to its pre-partial, pre-flood stage. I was exhausted, not hungry and vaguely disturbed. I longed in my soul for a regular rhythm; I wished I could do my yoga to get some distance, to detach; I missed Ms. Bank V.P. *By nature*, I thought, *I am so not a Fran.*

"You'll feel terrible, worse than you ever have, but you can get through it," Fran was saying when another nurse came in to tell her that Mrs. B.'s bed had to be changed because of an accident. As they went off together I heard Fran say, "I don't mean that

I shouldn't go to Mrs. B., but in the future might I suggest..."

I was alone and afraid and suddenly realized, I had every reason to be afraid: The cells in the lump in my breast had been malignant, "adenocarcinoma," the surgeon had said, and two thirds of the lymph nodes had been positive, too. I was facing some heavy-duty chemotherapy and things probably would not be all right for quite some time, if ever.

"Fran has something right," I sighed as I pushed away the overbed table and reached over for the fresh pillowcase to put on my pillow, "it's time I faced it."

I stood up and retrieved my water pitcher from the window sill and looked out for a minute. *There's one thing I know already,* I thought, *and that is that I am not going to wear a wig. Never can stand the things on others. So unnatural. Wouldn't want the tightness around my head and, I hear they are hot and itchy. No thank you. Probably not a prosthesis either. Way too restrictive, I* mumbled rebelliously aloud, "*I hate tight things around my chest; that's mainly why I haven't worn a bra for some time already. So what if people know that I have just one breast.*"

Though not again assigned to my care, Fran has stopped by each day since. Like a real sister, she sits on my bed and says, "I am in the other zone today but I came over because there are a few more things I want to tell you. Chemotherapy can give you intestinal cramps and looseness, you know what I mean, be sure to ask for medicine for that. Don't suffer more than you have to. My sister..."

Chapter Three

"Damned Liar of a Doctor"

FRAN DIDN'T HAVE ONE DETAIL QUITE RIGHT about the loss of my hair while on chemo. She said I would be standing in the shower some day with a clump of hair in my hand. Wish it were so. It is more like having a sticky web of wet hair wrapped around each individual finger and it is really, really hard to get off. When I rinse it off with water, the hair covers the drain. This has been going on for days in my case. Loose hair is everywhere: on my pillows, my sheets, the bathroom floor, my collars, in my mouth and on my plates. The wool hats I wear to keep warm in the cold of winter are lined with hair. I had no idea it would be this much work to contain so many thousands of single hairs! The daily compulsive behavior of picking them up reminds me of Grace who used to be one of my neighbors before she died of breast cancer. Remembering her gives me a clear and sober perspective of what might be my scenario, too.

Grace had a family history of breast cancer that should really be written in the textbooks. Every sister and every niece—I think there were seven or eight in all—died of the disease. Each had been painfully ripped away from Grace and she was openly and unashamedly bitter about it. She didn't know, she said, if she was an outcast or a heroine because she had lived to be eighty-six and had two healthy breasts.

But four summers ago she had felt the localized discomfort, the fear and then the lump. Grace came home after the mastectomy like a female version of Don Quixote, *The Man of La Mancha*. She waved her arm around in the air like a windmill and like those muscles in her arm weren't connected to her chest muscles at all. She told all of us neighbors that the doctor predicted that she would live well into her nineties. We could see that she was proud; proud, we thought, to be the toughest of all the women in her family.

Secretly, I believe, Grace had wondered if the other women in her family had really tried to stay alive. It had seemed to her so easy for all of them just to leave her, to leave her, to keep leaving her and to leave her all alone in the end just like her husband had done twenty-three years ago. Now, she knew. She was right to have been mad and disgusted with the whole lot of them all this time.

Grace did not say this but she might as well have. She was a tough old bird. A couple of summers before her diagnosis, I watched her wage war against a horde of wasps. Every day all day for two weeks she killed wasps. I would see her out there from my second story when I pushed open my bedroom curtain in the morning and she was still out there when I pulled it back after sundown. I do not know when or if she ate, drank or went to the bathroom.

The wasps had built a nest inside the walls of her house and they came and went through openings between the anchored sill and the cement foundation. Luckily, they had not found a way into her living quarters. When Grace discovered the wasps going in and out, she put on her fight'n—as they say in Maine—clothes. The first day and every day thereafter—as long as the war raged on—she wore a man's size navy and white handkerchief as a babushka, a blue, oversized man's shirt, a gathered, calf-length, gray-brown tweed skirt over heavy brown nylons, a pair of sturdy brown shoes, and a red, floral wrap-around, full-length apron. Thus outfitted, Grace—with a strategy for the war in mind—brought out her weaponry and advanced forthrightly into combat.

First, she used a straw broom. Like Ted Williams tagging one over the green monster at Fenway Park, she swung at and clobbered the wasps as they emerged from the foundation. With immediate follow-up chopping motions, she mercilessly whacked away at the stunned Sphecoidea—one of the superfamilies of wasps—on the concrete slab underfoot. Her assaults and possibly the wasps' cries for help alerted other wasps in the area. They—like loyal marines, *Semper Fi* and all that—swarmed towards their fallen comrades, giving Grace the opportunity to wallop and stun three or four more.

After a few days of these nonstop maneuvers, the binding of her broom gave way and the straw bristles were flying free like a crazy woman's hair in the midst of a screaming fit. Unfettered, the broom couldn't deliver a deadly enough blow anymore; so, Grace bought a new one.

On the sixth day I strolled over and she and I stood and looked down on a couple hundred or so stunned or dead wasps. So far, said Grace, it had been a good day. Being loath to kill anything—ever since I had tried to cut off a chicken's head but had squeezed my eyes shut at the last second spelling disaster for both the chicken and me—I bent down to get a better look at the struggling, segmented creatures. The more able were wrapping themselves around the lesser able and tugging at them. It was evident they were trying to nudge their fallen friends back into life and flight. I was touched. I remarked about how incredible their caring about one another was but Grace was disinterested. She was talking over me, fast, seemingly without stopping to take a breath, about how they just kept coming and coming.

What have they ever done to her? I wondered. *They mean her no harm. Not a single one has stung her in all these days of abuse and killing. Amazing!*

It's as if each wasp symbolizes some wrong done to her in her eighty-four years. Whack! That one was for Emily and here's one for Marcie and another for Genevieve. Take that, you stinging, sucking, six-legged, arthropod who knows nothing but to take, take and take from me! Nothing. Nothing is going to get to me or to my house. Not now, not ever! I am going to wipe you all clean off the frigg'n planet! And then I wondered idly if Grace used real swear words in her internal diatribes

After a week, Grace was on her third unfettered broom and was either discouraged or encouraged—I couldn't tell which. Whatever it was, it caused her to change tactics. With boards, hammer and nails she set to work blocking the entry and exit cracks between the sill and foundation. However, that did nothing to deter the stubborn enemy; they were too small and could squeeze through the tiniest of openings. She removed the boards.

Next maneuver, she brought out a bucket of tar, set it on fire and smoke billowed forth. She placed the smoking bucket against the house and for the next few days stood guard with her broom hoping the pests would come swarming out. No such luck.

On day Fourteen she had no choice but to go for chemical warfare. "I bought a 'big bomb,'" she told me. *More like a grenade actually*, I thought, as I looked at the pesticide-laden canister. She pulled the nails out of one end of some siding boards and propped them open with blocks of wood. Then, she worked the bomb into the opening and pulled the pin. It didn't explode—which all of us neighbors might have enjoyed—it would have broken the tension at least. It just slowly released its deadly gases into all the crevices.

A week later she had a couple of insulation and siding guys seal up every possible crack. She claimed it was to winterize the north side of the house, but she had lived in that house by herself through twenty freezing Maine winters. No doubt about it, Grace just wanted to seal the deal. She had won the war and vanquished the invaders! One had to admire that kind of spunk.

Four months after Grace's mastectomy surgery, that "damned liar of a doctor"—yes, I learned then, Grace did in fact swear—opened her up again and said it was "no use." The cancer was "everywhere." He had decided that she did not need radiation or chemotherapy at the time of her mastectomy, and then it was too late. I could well imagine that he thought: *this old crow of a woman, who talks my ear off, is probably ready to turn it in anyway; why make her miserable by giving her chemotherapy?* But why lie to her about living well into her nineties? The bum! Who gave him the right?

After that, Grace's fighting spirit was slowly but surely smothered to death. Her son and daughter-in-law, whom she had told me she never liked, moved in with her and it became eerily quiet. They didn't even seem to put out any garbage or walk to the mailbox to check if Grace had any cards or bills. When I called to ask if I could visit, they'd say, "She's resting."

One day from my second story window, I saw some litter on her lawn. She cared a lot about that huge lawn and always mowed it herself. I walked downstairs to remove the litter, and when I bent down to pick it up, I felt like I was trying to nudge her spirit back to life like the wasps had done for one another. I knew it wasn't going to happen. I knew her spirit had been broken and she was well on her way to following in the footsteps of her sisters, nieces and so many other women with breast cancer.

She died two weeks before Christmas in a heavy fog and I will admit that I was relieved it was over. The relatives emptied out the house and sold it in record time. Just like that, every trace of Grace was gone.

Now, with my hairs plugging the drain and remembering Grace, I know what I have to do. Like a Buddhist monk, I have to get all of my hair cut down to an eighth of an inch and I have to tell my mother that she has to fly back home to Montana. As much as she says she wants to take care of me, I can not let it happen. This is my fight, not hers, and I cannot take care of her need to appear useful. I am going to need all the time and space I can get to focus on winning my war my way. It is my turn to tilt at windmills, and like Grace and those before her, I, too, will *Dream the Impossible Dream.*

Chapter Four

Tragedies, Talents and Tangles

FOR TWENTY YEARS OR SO before this one, 1992, from the end of May to the end of September, Sophia's mother, Alexandra Charalambopoulou-Kellis-Huff—affectionately known as Mumma to me and to everyone in her family—would come to the coast of Maine to stay at the house of her son, Basil. She so loved and cherished the refreshing ocean air, the taste of fresh haddock and the long walks along the seashore on Ocean Avenue. She would walk all the way from Moody Point to the little grocery past Mile Road to get her Juicy Fruit chewing gum and her Pringles potato chips. Sadly though, this summer Mumma has come for only two weeks; it is a vacation for her from the Maneogian Nursing Home in Southgate, Michigan.

Mummer—the Downeast version of Mumma—has what has been diagnosed as second stage Alzheimer's disease. Roughly speaking, she has been losing her mental capacities for the last ten years or so and, being in the second of three stages, means that her mental changes have reached a critical point: she gets lost in familiar surroundings, she is confused by events, time and place and no longer can recall conversations, decisions or actions taken. It is so sad.

We would see her religiously working on her word search puzzles on Basil's front porch and think she was doing just fine; that was until we looked in the word search book. She and we blamed her eyesight when she no longer could thread a needle, and we said she had cooked enough in her life anyway when she didn't want to make a certain favorite Greek dish.   Eventually though, the denial in all of us broke down and her difficulties ever increasingly tugged at our hearts. In these two weeks this summer, they are tearing our hearts right out of our chests.

As Sophia's partner, I have participated in only this last slice of Mummer's life, and discovered over the years that the more she lost her mental abilities, the more she and I became simpatico. We loved to laugh when we were together. We would sit on the back porch of my house and I would draw her pictures of body parts, a few of the private body parts included, and she would laugh conspiratorially when she told me the Greek word for it. Chest? *Stithos.* Breast? *Veezee* for one, *veeza* for two. Buns? *Peeseeno or collisno.* She couldn't decide exactly which word and who cared if it wasn't correct? I was, still am, her unabashed adoring fan, a spellbound member of an audience at a one-woman show.

Because of the wretched disease with its attending dissolution of time boundaries such as current and past, and because of Mummer being a talkative, story-telling Greek who still had a firm grasp on dramatics, she told and retold, acted and reenacted all of her life's stories. Like a trout with my mouth wide open for the bait, I took them all in: hook, line and sinker. It became my self-appointed duty to honor her stories, to be her memory.

She still knows this: "I was born in Aegeon, Greece, on December 10, 1910. December 10, 1910." She emphasizes each word with short chops of one of her beautiful unblemished olive-skinned hands and is stunned to hear from me that this translates into her being 82 years old.

"Naw, not me, Sollod," she remonstrates as she turns to one of her daughters, Louise or Sophia, and asks with agonizing incredulity, "Am I?"

I was still using my Americanized name, Charlotte, back then and Mummer just could not wrap her head around that name. She settled on calling me Sollod and I said, "Close enough, Mumma." She called me other things in Greek, I know, but I didn't care. As long as her eyes were twinkling, and they always were, I knew it wasn't too bad. I was lucky; Basil's wife, Joy, wasn't. Nobody needed a translation when Mummer was unhappy with daughter-in-law. She would come over and tell Sophia all about the latest outrage in fluent, punctuated Greek with hand gestures throughout.

At Alexandra's terribly tender age of three, she used to tell me, her mother up and left her, her younger brother, her two older sisters and her father, all of them, to run away with another man. Her mother, according to Alexandra, was never seen nor heard from again. That painful beginning explained her often expressed and vehement dislike of cheap women. *"Poly fromma!"* she would say with obvious disgust. Then she would theatrically and spit-lessly spit, making the sound like she was really doing it, towards the ground at the sight of a barely-clad floozie, or some woman who was draping herself all over a man.

The young brother died of "grief," as Mummer remembered it, and not much later one sister died of tuberculosis and then the other died, too—of what, she did not know. Her father, she would frown sadly, was from then on a broken man and Alexandra had to live with her father's brother and his wife. She remembered being given a little "*mavro yataki*," a black kitten, which she would take to bed with her.

"It was so nice and soft and I love it," she cooed in reverie as she always cradled the imaginary kitten in her supple hands, brought them to her chest and swayed gently.

But this supposedly sweet story—meant to soothe—turned sad, also. "One night," Mumma would say, tsk-tsking softly with eyes closed and shaking her head side to side. "One night I roll over and in the morning I see the nice kitten flat and not alive!" She'd throw up her hands in anguish. "I lay on it in my sleeping!" she'd cry. There were always tears in her open eyes. "Oh, oh," she would moan, "I cry. I cry and cry for the kitten. I feel bad for a long, long time after. I cry, so much I cry!" She sobs inconsolably now, too, in its retelling.

I have listened to that story and have seen and heard her sadness so many times; yet, each and every time it is as if it were the morning after the tragedy for her, and each and every time her heart breaks anew. It is not easy to watch, but I do, hypnotized.

Ever since I was thirteen and for two years following when I had to watch my father die slowly of cancer, I have had a need to fix people and things—at least to try—and I wanted to fix Mummer, too, at first. *If I listen attentively to Mummer one more time*, I thought, *maybe it will ease her pain.* But I learned that this sadness of Mummer's is not fixable. That she does not retell and relive it in order for it to get fixed. Intellectually, I know that and I know that much of life is not fair or fixable and that there are lots of reasons for crying. But does that make her soul-sadness easier for me to see and hear? Not a bit. I stood by—and still do—helpless, wishing. Wishing her tears would be fewer, wishing I could hug them away, wishing I would no longer see myself as a fixer but only as an unabashed adoring fan. Mummer has never—and not now at this late date—given me any other role to play. It needs to be enough.

"I'm so sorry, Mumma; I'm so sorry."

"Old women, dress all in black," she would insist, "tell me things of dragons and monsters in chains coming up from the sea. They make noise: drugga, drugga, drugga! I so scared, drugga, drugga, drugga, at night."

There was urgency in her telling me this as if she needed to convince me of the truth of it.

"I believe you, Mumma, I believe you." Monsters of the past and thunder storms regularly set off terror in her tender soul. She wakes up at night now many, many times, confused, disoriented, shaking with fear, sobbing, sobbing, "God, forgive me, forgive me! I almost die! No mother! No father!"

It is a hopeless chore to soothe her in the hours of darkness this summer. Her daughters exhaust themselves. But with the beginning light of dawn, Mummer's anxieties and despair abate. Shortly after, she falls into a deep sleep. Upon awakening refreshed, Mummer, seemingly, has no memory of the difficult night gone by. On the other hand, her daughters—cursed, one might say in this instance, with intact short-term memories—will not soon forget.

Music, blessedly, was and still is a balm for Mummer's pain and grief. In her teen years and well beyond, the mandolin and guitar were her constant companions. She, the story goes, played with special talent and elegance.

"Oh, Sollod, I play so beautiful," she would recall and I would watch as she squeezed her eyes shut, held the fingers of both hands together up near but not touching her smooth cheeks and slightly shook her head as one might do in describing a deliciously delicate wine. She still has very few wrinkles in that wonderfully expressive face which is framed by lovely, still-thick, salt and pepper hair.

"Sooooo beautiful," she would repeat with an innocent and obvious deep appreciation of her gift.

Alexandra no longer plays the instruments but when she hears the sharp, metallic sound of the bouzouki—the mainstay of the vibrant rhythm of the Greek folk dance—her mind pulls away from tragedy. She lifts her right knee, then her right hand and she transitions her whole being into the beat. Her timing is flawless and it is evident that the origin and memory of the dance comes from somewhere other than her troubled and tangled brain. She dances and dances holding hands and arms up in the air and clasping onto other hands and arms in the air and then she throws her head back and laughs with unrestricted joy and delight. "Opa!" "Opa!"

"I cannot do more," she says breathlessly as she comes to sit next to me and pounds her fist on her knee. "No, really, they put plastic knee in here. Oh, darn it! I no want it. Numb, always numb. No feeling!"

When twenty years old Alexandra was able to purchase a sewing machine and, with practice, soon became an excellent seamstress. Neighbors recognized her skills and brought projects for her to do. She was pleased to finally earn her keep in the home of her uncle and aunt. Later, in Maine, she worked for C. M. Almy Company, a small sewing factory; her specialty was sewing vestments for parish priests.

"One dollah, one dollah only! For a day of sewing!" she would remember, pursing her lips and thrusting one hand forward angrily. The women employees, she said, were rigidly timed, too, including the frequency and length of bathroom breaks. Mumma would tell me with her head held high that they walked as one—she might as well have said marched or protested—and were given a ten cent raise.

"Good for you, Mummer! Good for you!" I would applaud boisterously—imagining her as my own Greek version of Crystal Lee Sutton, the now famous textile worker and union organizer, whose life and bravery I had seen depicted by Sally Fields in the movie, "Norma Rae." Each retelling, Mummer would take a bow with a big smile on her face.

"Bravo!" she'd say. "Bravo!" She was so proud of what they had accomplished.

"But ten cents only!" she would exclaim with a forced exhalation through tight lips to underline her disgust. "He say, 'ten cents. I give you ten cents more.' Aw, money, money. *Hremata*," she'd say shaking her head woefully and moving her thumb rapidly over the fingertips of the same hand. "*Hremata* not good, Sollod. Cause all kinda problems."

One day at the age of twenty-two, Alexandra, was walking on a street in Aegeon, Greece, when unbeknownst to her a man fourteen years her senior selected her to be his bride. Louis Kellis, a trim, wiry, determined Greek man from Asia Minor—Mummer endearingly and innocently always referred to it as "Aunt Jemima"—had fought in a Turkish war, had seen his parents beheaded when he chanced to look backward in escape and had immigrated to America. From Ellis Island, New York, he made his way to Fairfield, Maine. Where, he had been told, he would find a Greek community. This he found to be true and soon after established his own residence in the town of nearby Pittsfield, Maine.   Louis
enlisted and fought in World War I, after which, he returned to Greece and brought his two brothers, Mike and Tony, back to Pittsfield with him. They

each bought a home near Louis' place. Later, the three brothers went back together and brought their only remaining sibling, Mercena, a sister, over as well. Finally, when his family was secure and when it became financially possible, Louis traveled a third time to Greece to find himself a Greek wife.

Upon request, Alexandra's uncle gave Louis the go-ahead for the marriage and within three weeks Alexandra was married to a complete stranger, terribly sea-sick on a ship on the North Atlantic Ocean and headed for God knows where. "What I do? I know nothing," she would wail. "I cry; I cry!"

Naïve and not understanding or speaking a word of English, she solemnly vouched to me each time in the retelling, that she cried the entire first two years of their marriage.

"Two whole years, Mumma?"

Louis kept getting her pregnant, she was certain, to keep her busy and to take her mind off her loneliness. With this man everyone called "Louie" she had four live children plus a miscarriage within a span of seven years.

"My pregnancies go on forever!"

Mumma's eyes would roll up to her forehead as she slouched in her chair with feigned exhaustion. The first two children were, as Mummer described it, "very long and stretched and kicked" her belly. Because of it, these days, as a security blanket, no matter what the summer heat and humidity may be—we don't know how she stands it—she wears her pantyhose pulled up high, often two pairs, plus her snuggies (long underwear) to "keep it all in place."

Over time Louie taught Alexandra what he knew of cooking and he found the cookbook, Can The Greeks Cook! With translation help, she learned to cook delicious lamb stew, chicken and rice soup (*kota soupa avgolemono*), stuffed grape leaves

31

(*dolmathes*), spinach pie (*spanikopita*), and all kinds of vegetables from the large garden of her brother-in-law, Mike. She taught herself to make *baklava, kourambiathes, koulourakia,* and other Greek pastries; the tantalizing aromas would waft through the neighborhood. They attracted hobos from the neighboring rail yard who came to her back door and asked for a bite to eat—she denied no one—and friends of the children loved to congregate in her kitchen.

Louie worked long, hard hours as a loomer in the textile mills in Pittsfield. It was the Great Depression and members of the family had to stand in long lines to get rations of eggs, margarine and sugar; the children picked beans and dandelion greens; the guys hunted and fished. To supplement his wages, Louis drove a taxi, participated in boxing matches, ran a small neighborhood grocery and sold hot dogs and peanuts at local football games. When the World War II effort began, he sometimes worked twenty-four hours a day making woolen blankets for the soldiers.

Alexandra would tell me of how she pleaded with him: "Louie, Louie, you no eat, you no sleep, you get sick!"

"Louie would say to me, '*Agape mou*, dawlin, dawlin,'" and, she added, "he would kiss me gently."

Mummer would make sweet kissing sounds through puckered lips as she told me this. Eyes closed, hands cupping her face, it was easy to see that she was desperately wanting to recall his manly scent, the taste and feel of him—or was she in actuality recalling them? It was so hard to know what she did or did not recall. Were they just stories and imaginings, scenes as if in a play, or could she still actually bring those precious memories back? Can any of us? What was clear to me was that she had, at some point, fallen head over heels in love with the stranger called Louie.

Before long, Louis did get sick. He was diagnosed at the Veterans Hospital in Augusta with a cancerous kidney tumor. After two long years of suffering, the last three months of which he spent in the hospital, Louis died, leaving Alexandra to care for herself and the four children aged five through thirteen.

"Terrible, terrible, Sollod," Mummer would always moan and more tears from that immense aching void would flow down her grief-stricken face. Her hands would twist, fold and unfold the white, cotton handkerchief in gestures of despair. "I cry. I cry."

Sophia remembers her mother back then taking to her bed and calling the children to her side. "I, too, want to die!" she had cried.

Mummer would tell me, "In tears and on my knees I pray to God by my bed. 'Give me strength Lord to take care of these children! Four children, Lord!'"

"It's true, I tell you, Sollod, I feel strength come into my hands." She would hold her hands in a tight fist and then continue, "My wrists, up my arms and all through my body!"

She would follow the flow of energy she was describing to me by opening her hands and moving one hand up the surface of the other hand, wrist and arm and over the front of her body and then would strike a reverent pose: hands folded and quietly holding the handkerchief, head nodding to affirm her truth. I confess; I became a convert. I am her believer.

The Greek Orthodox religion eventually sustained her. Every Sunday she took her children on the train to the Greek Church and community in Bangor and weekly, she recited verbatim each and every word of the Divine Liturgy including the priest and choir responses. She can still do so to this day even though she can't tell you what you or she said just two seconds ago and, if left alone, would wander and get lost. It won't be too long before she won't know who we are but I bet she'll still know the liturgy.

I don't know if I will see Mumma again after these two weeks. I'm sure that she won't be able to stay over at Basil's again; it is too difficult for the family, and I doubt if I will be able to travel to Michigan because of the toll the chemotherapy has taken on my lungs. I'll miss her a lot. In fact, I miss her already during those times when she is so into her confusion. Thankfully, though, she is still here with us part of the time.

"Where, where all this water come from? How God make this so much? How he make universe?" Mummer asks deeply perplexed, sweeping her arm over the expanse of the ocean. She traces the face of the man in the moon and she looks deeply into the eyes of her great grandchild.

"Hello, dawlin. So cute," she says making tiny "tch, tch" sounds.

She teases her adult children, reaches up to pull the ear lobe of her successful son, the lawyer. With a mischievous wink to me, she comically mimics the sternness of her daughters behind their backs. Like a kid, I delight in her laughter and playfulness.

When I ask and when I work hard to keep her attention, she still teaches me: *patellutha* for butterfly, *yenecka* for woman. Yesterday, while organizing and reorganizing the many napkins and lifesavers in her well-worn purse for the umpteenth time, she said mournfully, "I don't want to go, to go up, to die."

I saw the troubled emotion in her pretty hazel eyes and as I took her precious hand, I responded with, "I don't either, Mumma. I don't want to go either. Not today, anyway."

She repeated my words slowly. "Not today anyway." I could see she was pondering the meaning.

After a bit, my brave heroine, my teacher, good friend and playmate smiled broadly up at me, clapped me soundly on my shoulder and called out, "Bravo, Sollod! Not today. Bravo!"

And Stories from Arizona

Chapter Five

In Desperate Need of a Guardian

My mammograms have been normal for five years—since 1987—and there have been no signs of recurrence of breast cancer anywhere in my body. I am faithful in my monthly self breast exams, including deep into my armpits, and, thank goodness, have no further follow-up with my personality-deficient oncologist—Fran had been so right about him, bless her heart. Now, when the raw, cold winds of late autumn hit each year, I leave my home in Wells, Maine, and fly by commercial airlines to a trailer park here in sunny, still quite hot, Mesa, Arizona. For five to six months I try to adapt to living in a 12' by 35' park model trailer in the desert. In mid-spring I reverse the process and go back to the ocean and the refreshing salt air. I am not even fifty years old and already I am in my third winter as a snowbird. "So many snowbirds: so little freezer space," the bumper sticker slogan says here in Arizona.

This premature retirement of mine was, unfortunately, not precipitated by premature amassed wealth—as it is with quite a number of baby boomers these days. Those lucky fair-weather fowls retire early and flock with their peers to posh resort areas. No, my precipitous retirement is due to my genetically impaired liver. A mutation in my DNA—passed down from one individual through multiple generations and to me—results in my liver being unable to secrete enough of the protective enzyme known as Alpha 1 Antitrypsin into my blood stream. An insufficient supply of this enzyme coming to my lungs results in constant damage being done to my alveoli, the tiny little air sacs in my lungs. The end result is similar to what happens with smoking: chronic bronchitis, emphysema and, in many folks, asthma.

I was already restricted to a moderate degree in my activities before the chemotherapy but when healthy cells were destroyed in my body along with the deadly cancer cells—as is the way with chemotherapy—it really brought my respiratory capacity down, so far down that I qualified for disability. Needless to say, I am no longer a faculty member—they refused to give me tenure but, thank God, my disability was granted in my "terminal year" (their words, not mine) and so I still have the university's health benefits. Also, I no longer do well in cold weather. Consequently, I seek the warmer, dryer climate to keep functioning best I can as do thousands and thousands of retired seniors 20-30 years older than I. In the beginning it was tough because—and it was a sober fact to face—for the most part, the pace of seniors is not my pace. I cannot do as much nor, go as fast.

During the first two winters, I scrambled about securing my trailer, doing a bit of interior decorating, finding Pulmonary Associates in Phoenix to secure a doctor and at which I would be getting my weekly intravenous infusions—I get a pooled plasma product with a high concentration of the enzyme that is lacking in my system—the hospital just in case, the library and generally getting the lay of the land. In other words, I avoided getting involved. However, this third winter—I had firmly resolved—*this* winter I would seek new friends and develop new skills. It was time. It was time that I accepted my disabled retired life amongst oldsters in the Southwest. Like it or not.

The options were somewhat overwhelming at first. In retrospect, it would have been helpful, of course, to have had a knowledgeable person in my corner, a discerning, sensitive soul, for instance, who could have advised me on the pitfalls of being viewed as a gullible tourist-type. But, no, I knew no such person. I had to sort through the offerings on my own, and from studying the flyers hanging in the breezeway, I could see that there was a lot going on in the park. One could golf, bowl, square, round or line dance, clog, play shuffleboard, throw horseshoes, swim, hike or bike. Except for some limited swimming—which is easier for me because my lungs are hyper inflated so that I float like a buoy—those activities were all out of my range. I looked instead then at something more sedentary. Zipper art, tole or T-shirt painting and card games such as bridge, poker and pinochle didn't interest me. The computer and photography clubs intrigued me but my brother—whose genetics and lungs are like mine—excels in those. Woodcarving appealed to me, too, but Sophia—who has lupus and who doesn't do well in cold weather either—is into that. *This winter*, I remember thinking, *it is important that I not be enmeshed, that I do it on my own. So those three areas are out.*

I finally decided on the Kachina Doll Class taught by someone named Betty Campbell. I remembered reading in a brochure that the Heard Museum in Phoenix had quite a collection of these dolls. "A Kachina doll," I had read, "is a likeness of an impersonated Hopi spiritual guardian." That had piqued my interest. And I had also seen a few Kachina dolls for sale in places; I had been attracted to the creativity involved in making them. I loved their colors and natural garb. In fact, I must have already made a sort of mental commitment to this class because all last summer I was surreptitiously picking up feathers, bits of drift wood and shells on the Atlantic shoreline. My collection filled a small box, and, as I wrote my name on the attendance list, I could easily imagine the wonderful healing earth mothers that I would create.

Darn it all! In December I was in the grips of a lingering flu, and I had to miss my first class. For the second class, due to a longer-than-planned appointment, I arrived an hour late.

"Never mind," said take-charge-instructor, Betty—who was a middle-aged Caucasian and not a Hopi or any other kind of Native American from what I could see, "I'll make a body for you. You can coat it at home this week and we'll get you going on the clothes, too."

She quickly cut assorted pieces of Styrofoam from long tubes of various thicknesses for the limbs and added a round Styrofoam ball for the head. Hurriedly and expertly, she crafted a unisex body by welding pieces together with lots of toothpicks soaked in glue and inserted at various angles. Then, she deftly snipped off the protruding toothpick ends. "Tacky glue, which you can get at any fabric or craft shop, dries very quickly," she explained. She handed me the white, feature-less, naked body and gave me a sheet of instructions along with a plastic baggie full of a white powder. "The powder is a plaster-like compound that you add water to and it dries hard like porcelain. You'll need to put on multiple coatings and use this sandpaper in between each coating," she instructed. This was followed by a varnish-like substance in a Gerber's baby food jar "for a last sealer coat," flesh and mustard-colored paints, one brush, patterns and bits of cloth and leather for the clothes and said, "I'll bring you your own paints and brushes next week." That signaled the end of class.

I smiled at my classmates who, I noticed, were all painting identical designs on their dolls and clothing. Next week maybe, I thought, we'll introduce ourselves.

During the week, midst Christmas decorations, cards, and gifts—and with persisting coughing spasms—I coated, sanded, coated, sanded, coated, sanded and put on two layers of the sealer coat. My unisex body now looked like one of those featureless extraterrestrials. Then, per instructions, I painted the head antique gold and the body the deep flesh color. I cut out pieces of clothing: a soft leather loin cloth with flaps front and back, wrist and arm bands, parts to make high suede boots and an over the shoulder Miss America type sash. I have not worked that hard since I had to read and grade forty term papers in one weekend with brand new bifocals!

In the third class—I was stunned to learn it was only a four-class-per-Kachina cycle—I hesitantly and self-consciously presented my coated, painted but naked, Kachina body for review. The other five attendees, all women, were impressed with how well I had done. They smiled and said so. I was pleased as punch. *I don't know what I had been getting freaked out about*, I thought. *This retired, senior citizen thing could turn out to be a lot of fun.* In that class and the one remaining we painted intricate designs on the body and on the clothes. So intricate and detailed were the designs that I had to wear a head apparatus with a magnifying glass over my bifocals in order to see what I was doing and a paint brush that had only three bristles. My neck has been sore ever since. We added beads and fur. The teacher gave me more paints, brushes and a bill at the end. I was astonished to see that I owed her $74.00!

"It costs more at first when you build up your supplies," said Betty nonchalantly. The second doll cost me $51.00.

"I know what I'll do," I rationalized to Sophia; "I'll get an extra kit for each doll. The kits cost about $25.00 each; then I'll keep one doll and sell the duplicate. That way I should be able to recoup the money I've had to pay out."

"Are you going to use the things that you brought from Maine?" Soph asked.

"Not really," I said, saddened by the realization that every line and every color is prescribed by the Native Americans and that I will not be producing any original earth mothers. "Betty says, 'For the Kachina doll to be authentic, one must follow the Native American prescriptions exactly.' It doesn't seem to matter to her, strangely enough though, that the real Hopi Kachina doll is carved from wood and ours are made with Styrofoam."

This past week it all came crashing down on me. I overheard veteran student, Jane—we never did introduce ourselves; I have learned some names by listening—and Betty talk about some Kachina dolls that the student had seen at an Indian Trading Post.

"I hope that you didn't tell them that you make Kachinas!" Teacher laughed heartily as she talked. "They frown on us non-Indians making them, you know."

Really? Who knew? Oh, right, this is the same woman, I mused, who was irate last week that the city officials had agreed to change the new wall markings at Sky Harbor Airport. The African-Americans had been protesting that the markings looked like the KKK of the Ku Klux Klan.

"Everybody just wants too much these days!" she had announced determinedly and most of the class had concurred in their murmurings. I am not proud to say it but I sat dumbly silent.

Now, believe me when I say that I am sick at heart. I am a hippie really, a child of the sixties. As such, I love to belt out the words to the song, "When you are going to San Francisco, remember to wear a flower in your hair; when you go to San Francisco, you are going to meet some gentle people there..." I participated in, even facilitated, racial awareness workshops in a Psychiatric Staff Development Department. I am excited by the new Democratic administration. The word liberal doesn't frighten me and, yes, there was a time in my life when I was a card-carrying American Civil Liberties Union member—I still would be if I could afford it. I've been oppressed—to reiterate, I was a non-English speaking immigrant and am unusually tall, some would say abnormally tall, plus I prefer women—so I know about being in the minority status. And, here I am, totally, embarrassingly politically incorrect, sitting in my Kachina Doll Class with enough coating material, paints and clothing/accessory kits to do a minimum of six more Styrofoam bodies! What was I thinking?

How pathetic. I could have used the money to fix the hole in my roof because it has been leaking since New Year's Day and it has been leaving yellow rings on my white ceiling tiles. Nobody told me that it could rain for 16 days straight here in the desert! El Nino, La Nina, whatever. Man, could I ever use a spiritual guardian, impersonated or not, for this snowbird business!

Chapter Six

That Old, Old Story

MARLENE, A LONG TIME FRIEND OF SOPHIA—Marlene was Sophia's first head nurse when the two worked at the old Sisters' Hospital back in Waterville, Maine—and thereby now a quasi-friend of mine, says, "Yes!" to the Christmas season and all that it entails. She is like a kid who claps nonstop, jumps up and down and hollers with exaggerated enthusiasm, "Yes! Yes!" Marlene decorates, bakes, sends packages of homemade turtles, shops, sends more packages and generally is happy from Thanksgiving until the day after Christmas when at last her immune system relaxes and she comes down with a sore throat and a cold.

Her season of unbridled happiness always includes attending a performance of Tchaikovsky's Russian ballet, *The Nutcracker*. Marlene attends every single year and last year simply could not believe that I had lived a half century without ever having seen even one performance. Where had I been all my life?! Marlene—retired but still a head nurse kind of a person—immediately vowed to remedy this profound deficiency of mine. So—exercising the lesson learned by Jack Nicholson's character in the movie "One Flew over the Cuckoo Nest," i.e., do not go up against a determined head nurse—and ever wanting to be acculturated to America's time-honored traditions, I accepted Marlene's invitation to attend this year's performance of *The Nutcracker* in Chandler, Arizona. Sophia accompanied us.

As Soph and I waited for Marlene to park the car and for the doors of the Chandler Building of the Performing Arts to open, I enjoyed seeing an extreme range in fashions. All apparently permissible and modeled by young and old alike, it went from sweats and tennies to spiked heels and evening dresses, from skin-tight tops and equally tight pants pulled all the way up—and not showing any panty lines—to oversized tops advertising the Phoenix area sports teams and pants pulled down below a decent level. Pairings of parent and child clearly demonstrated the old saying, *like father like son*; and more evident in this case, *like mother like daughter*. Regardless of dress and age, I could see that the children were keenly anticipating this event and that they were obviously no strangers to ballet. Everywhere, youngsters were attempting to plie, leap about and pirouette.

The first half of *The Nutcracker* was performed by mostly young dancers. This, Marlene informed us in a whisper, was somewhat unusual, but, she said, "it's all coming off without a flaw." I was enchanted as millions before me have been. Truly, the over-the-top red and pink pageantry was grand, the creativity on display in the sets and costumes was awe-inspiring and to watch the boundless energy of so many diverse kids being channeled into a constructive community activity was totally affirming. Unfortunately, however, I had a decisively negative reaction to one thing: each boy child in the story was given a Christmas present of a life-like, wooden rifle. Mind you, I am not talking about the rifles of the wooden soldiers; I am talking about the Christmas gifts of rifles. That disturbed and angered me.

During the intermission I told Marlene, in response to her asking if I was enjoying myself, that the performers were charming, the set wonderful, the seat and leg room great and, yes, I was having a good time. I thanked her for inviting us, for getting the tickets well in advance and for driving.

She beamed and said, "I told you you'd love it!"

"I am surprised though," I said philosophically, "that in this day and age, with all the violence and especially the shootings in schools like in Columbine, that they give such young boys those rifles as Christmas presents. They looked so real; I would have thought that they could give them something like a ball, a bat, glove or a game."

"This is a fairy tale, Tjaakje, an old fairy tale," replied Marlene curtly as we both watched tiny tykes all around us try to rise higher up on their toes or to march a stiff-kneed step.

"I realize that," I reflected, "but, nonetheless, it is clear to me that all these kids here in the audience are mimicking the performers, and why a gun?"

Sophia was giving me her forced, tight, little smile and Marlene was tensing up.

"It's not that I'm not enjoying myself," I hastened to amend; "I am."

"Violence happens everywhere and always has and probably always will," Marlene bristled. "You can't let that spoil this story! It's an old, old story. Lighten up, Tjaak!"

This having been said, she turned decisively away from me. There was no doubt in anyone's mind: it was her final word on the issue.

Thankfully, the lights were lowering and no further conversation was required. We returned to our seats where I sighed out my stress and frustration a few times as excited children all around settled back into their seats. Sophia surreptitiously pressed my hand.

"I hear you but you can't change her," she whispered into my ear.

"I know," I nodded and sighed some more as darkness engulfed us. Once the curtains opened for the second half, I hoped, I would once again be swept away by sugar plum fairies and such. Only, a part of me, I realized reflectively, is never completely swept away. A part of me is always on alert.

Most people will say that it is unbelievable, unfathomable, children shooting children. Not me. I think anything is fathomable. After all, I was born into unfathomable violence in the form of Adolph Hitler—and so many others who thought like him—in World War II. Thanks to them I spent my infancy and first two toddling years in a Nazi occupied village. My dad picked up pieces of a neighborhood child in a bucket, for heaven's sake. It must have been through the process of osmosis that I at that young age absorbed the ever-present threat of harm from one's fellow man. Clearly, the sight of a rifle and the knowledge of what that man with the rifle could do were imprinted on my brain through the soft fontanels of my skull.

When I was a little older kid in the supposedly safer United States, my brother, John, had a friend stay for an overnight. This kid aimed John's BB gun right at John and luckily it hit his belt buckle instead of his eye or his head. Lucky, too, that it was the BB gun and not the 22.

John shot magpies from our back steps every chance he got with Dad's 22 gauge rifle. I hated hearing it. Dad shot whatever bird or animal he decided needed killing. The fact that killing came so easily to them always bothered me.

Later, as an adult, Lee, a licensed psychiatric technician I knew, shot and killed Jane, his 32 year-old wife, with a handgun one summer day because she had left him. Just walked up to her door and shot her cold. She was a colleague of mine; we worked in the same department. Her office was two doors down and we spoke to one another every day.

They force children to become soldiers in Liberia and The Congo. Boys begin at the age of twelve to murder, maim and rape their own neighbors in order to get a meal from some rebel leader.

It ticks me off that we live day in and day out with people—face it, men and boys for the most part—killing each other and us females. Don't you see the blood, the lifeless eyes and the awkward position of the limbs every time you hear about it? I do.

I want people to believe and to fathom children shooting children, children killing each other, men killing children, a mother screaming and hot, steaming blood pouring out of holes. It happens all the time, every day, every minute.

I am certain that women are instrumental in performances such as *The Nutcracker*; they could make a difference. They could replace a rifle with a ball and glove. Is that really too much to ask?

But on the other hand, boys must be good little soldiers and they must grow up to be young men who would be ready to kill other young men who were also good little soldiers. They need to learn the killing business to defend power, territory or religion and to save helpless females—no matter what craziness is acted out here and there along the way or who gets killed by whom outside the parameters of war. It is never too soon to get kids ready for their part in this age old drama. Isn't that right? I get it; I really do. I wish I didn't. Marlene is correct: it is an old, old story and I for one am not ashamed to say that I am sick and tired of it.

Don't get me wrong; I am not a pacifist. I would like to be but I am realistic about the corruption that results from those having too much power: ignored by outsiders, it results in genocide. Same with the death penalty, I am against it but stop short of a complete ban. I wish we knew more about deterrence and what truly constitutes a danger to society. And the right to keep and bear arms? I agree; we should have the right, but I would not buy a gun nor have one anywhere near me. Way too dangerous.

What I object to primarily is the programming of the human race; teaching children to act in exactly the same way people have been acting *ad infinitum*. I think choices about killing and war should be made by adults. How will we ever make any progress in curbing the violence otherwise?

This fairy tale has turned into a hairy tale, I thought glumly still sitting in the dark waiting for the curtain to rise. *Christmas season or not, and call me a curmudgeon if you must, but I had hoped that we as a species were farther along than that.* Marlene, on the other hand, was leaning forward with eager anticipation. She continued—like every other moment during this December month—to be deliriously happy.

Chapter Seven

The Art of Small Talk

ON CHRISTMAS DAY, 1993, Sophia and I joined the other 250 or so Sunlife Trailer Resort residents and their visiting relatives in our spacious activity hall for a traditional holiday turkey dinner. Typical of my life experiences to date, I found the turkey and trimmings to be delicious, but the socializing in conjunction with the dinner to be a real pain. As usual (sigh) it had me feeling like an awkward adolescent all over again.

Unlike Sophia and me, nearly all the folks at our park are senior heterosexual couples. Predictably, the opening topic of conversation for them at our festive gathering was where their children were spending the holiday and what the weather was like where the children were. Childless, I stood by and smiled benignly. This particular smile is a sort of armor I have learned to put on in these situations.

A small percentage of the residents are widows and widowers. The ice breaker for members of this group was to share the time and cause of death of their dearly departed spouse as well as the number of years that the bereaved had now been alone on Christmas day. I demurely murmured my regrets.

I observed, however, that when a person shared that the spouse had left via divorce, the topic was politely dropped and the parties moved on to discuss the winter weather. I followed suit.

Then—and this is the primary source of my social awkwardness, of course—there is a minuscule percent, a few, a very precious few of us, like Sophia, me, and perhaps one, two, or a few more in the park, no one ever knows how many, who are of a different persuasion. We are the mysterious people. In the introductory phase of a conversation, as the curious souls chip away at bringing the details of our lives to light, the pride and dignity of us mysterious people are always at stake. This is where I inevitably begin to fumble.

I am not good at handling this beginning phase. I know this about myself. I see the warning sign clearly: LAND MINES AHEAD! It makes no difference. I bumble through the terrain, unskilled, setting off bombs.

For instance, at our special Christmas dinner this year, this is how it unfolded. Emily, a new resident, enthusiastically introduced herself to me. After peering at my name tag and swearing that she would never be able to pronounce my name, she asked, "Where is your husband?" Emily looked to either side of me, a little behind and around the immediate vicinity.

"He is not here," I replied concretely.

"Where is he then? Is he coming?"

"No, there is no husband."

"What happened to him?" Emily stubbornly persisted.

"Nothing. Nothing happened to him. I didn't marry."

"Never?"

"Never."

She turned to introduce me to her husband, who hovered just behind her left hip,

"Honey," she said, "Meet this woman. She has never had a man!"

I was sure that I had heard Emily verbally underscore the word *never*. It was so: I had never had a husband. But she had changed the word, *husband*, to *man*, and her misrepresentation really irritated me. I became instantly defensive.

"That's not exactly true," I retorted under my breath. "I've had men, sort of, well, more or less anyway. Several men."

My mind quickly reeled back to my teens, twenties and early thirties. We had gone through the sexual revolution and it was pre HIV and AIDS. Dating should have been easy, but I had gone through some awkward, awful, ambivalent, struggling dating times before I had come to my true lesbian self. I mentally listed my various male pursuers. The first was Maynard. I remember driving the tractor out in the field the next day with my shirt off to get a tan. I was feeling so exhilarated, singing at the top of my lungs; I was that happy. If he would have called me for a second date, I might have considered a heterosexual lifestyle.

The second was the butcher who had lost three of his fingers. He loved talking about how he had made the cut and the size of the blade, over and over again. It may not have been entirely an accident that I almost drowned in Lake Michigan while water-skiing on that date with him.

There was Ken, the milk toast Campus Crusade for Christ fellow who had all his ten fingers but no interesting stories to tell, ever. And the other Campus Crusade guy who was a Latino and eager to try his Latin wiles on me no matter what Christ might have said about it.

The shorter-than-me toad of a Psychiatric Resident who, after he kissed me while we were standing, shared this insightful discovery: "Now I know why you reminded me of my mother," he enthused. "She always looked down on me just the way you are!"

Also, there had been the sensitive artist, Bob, who softly traced and memorized my every line and curve—that was fun; the ever understanding, touchy-feely clinical psychology graduate student; and the priest who was by his own admission experimenting while in the process of deciding whether or not to abandon his celibacy vows.

Never to be outdone by the single stags, there were the multiple married men who, if I had concurred, would have blithely abandoned their wedding vows. I swear it was my long legs and long blonde hair that did it, not my come-hither looks or actions. I never knew how to do that feminine stuff. A female friend asked me once if I had any idea how seductive I was. No, I didn't. I didn't have a clue.

"I didn't want to marry a man," I announced resignedly to Emily and husband as he extended his hand and I extended mine.

"Nice to meet you, too," I said as I shook his hand, smiled, and nodded distractedly. Emily and husband nodded and smiled back. No one spoke.

And, I continued in thought, there was Jim, the no-strings-attached, free man, the "solitary man," as he called himself, who had my name on his life goals list for a not-so-solitary night—or so he hoped. Whom had I missed? And besides, I pondered, there is the definition of what "had" is and....

Emily, having lowered her bucket down into the well and come up empty, moved on. Hubby followed suit.

"Hello! Mrs. Sophia Kellis. Kellis is your married name, yes?"

"Yes," nodded Sophia affirmatively—obviously not as wedded to truth as I—as she adroitly side-stepped a repeat of my experience.

"What did you bring to the dinner, Emily? We brought the vegetables, squash and peas with onions, my favorites. Who do you think is the brave woman who baked the turkey? It looks great, doesn't it?"

Sophia smoothly asked and answered her own questions as she gently guided Emily over to survey their choices for dessert. Husband trailed after them, and I was left standing alone. Momentarily relieved of social pressure, I could not help but envy those who come with the gift for small talk. What was it about a particular developmental stage that has left me so socially deprived? I wondered.

Chapter Eight

Will the Real April Fool Please Stand Up

SOPHIA AND I CONCUR ON THIS MUCH: she is street smart and I am educated. For instance, Sophia will ask rhetorically, "How do you separate a kaegle from a fart?" and I will meticulously draw out and explain the pelvic musculature. Or, she'll come out in her purple boa and the matching purple veiled hat with little else on and say, "There is nothing worse than a wet pants and a tight bra!" She is wonderfully spontaneous, down to earth—she grows and feeds worms in her especially designed worm bin so she can use the castings on her vegetable garden, she is that down to earth—and has a great sense of humor.

That is not to say that she is not educated, because she is. She graduated from the Providence Hospital Diploma Program and is licensed as a Registered Nurse. Nor does it mean that I don't have street smart moments and that I don't appreciate the point of view of the street smart person because I very much do. In fact, for a number of years I taught a Leadership in Nursing course and in that course I honored one of Sophia's experiences in nursing to emphasize the value of being street smart.

At the end of each semester, my last piece of advice to the students in the class was always this: "Just because you now have all this textbook knowledge—and, trust me, you will use that knowledge—you will not find everything you will need to know in nursing in a textbook. In other words, what I am saying to you is that you should not summarily throw out what you have already learned in life. Nursing involves real life and real relationships."

"For example," I would say, "a friend of mine, Sophia, was working on a medical unit one evening and a couple of newly graduated and licensed nurses were totally flummoxed. An elderly male patient was unable to empty his bladder and needed to be catheterized but his penis, they said, was too shriveled and retracted. Neither of them had been able to grasp the penis in order to insert the catheter. 'Shall we call the doctor? Can he order a medication?' they inquired. 'Come with me,' Sophia instructed. They trailed her to the elderly gentleman's room and there she pulled back the bed linens. 'Watch carefully,' she said as she began gently, yet seductively, stroking the man's inner thigh. Sure enough, the penis started to grow. 'Now, grab that sucker!'"

I mention all this because Sophia, the spontaneous street smart woman, is surprisingly gullible when it comes to my April Fool's Day jokes and I, the cerebral one, can be amazingly ruthless in the jokes I spring on her. Go figure? One who is rational might think it would be the other way around, but no. For instance, the year when I was nearing the end of my chemotherapy I called her at six a.m. on April 1st and, quite unlike me, I feigned hysteria and sobs. I carried on about how all the stress had sent me into this sleepless, anxious mode and that I had felt this really strong urge to just run away. During the night, I burbled, I got in the car and drove south on the freeway with no idea of where I was going. Between sniffles and hiccups I told her that I was now in a MacDonald's on the outskirts of Hartford, Connecticut. That I had left Wells without a wallet or purse and that the car was out of gas. And, for good measure, I added that I even had to borrow the money to call her. "Can you come and help me?" I wailed piercingly.

She's Greek. She's the one with the drama genes, but, if I must say so myself, I am pretty sure I would have received an Oscar for that performance; I was that good.

"Now?" Sophia asked incredulously. "You want me to drive to Hartford, Connecticut, **now** at six o'clock in the morning? That is about six hours of driving from here!"

"I know," I cried; "I know; I'm so sorry but I don't know what else to do?"

"Can I at least take a shower first?" she asked. "And I'll have to eat some breakfast. What are you going to do before I get there?"

I allowed a little time to go by as I sniffled and blew my nose and then blurted out, "O, Syphie Lou, you are such an April Fool!"

Not too long ago I dragged myself home gasping for air and sweating profusely—so I made it appear anyway. It was brutally hot in Mesa on the 1st of April that year and I had driven myself to the hospital for my infusion.

"Soph!" I called hoarsely at the foot of the stairs leading up to the trailer. "Can you come out here?"

I explained between rasps and gasps how the van had overheated and had stalled in traffic down on Higley Street. "It's kind of in a precarious spot and really needs to be moved before a car hits it. I'm so sorry, but it was just too hot for me to stay in there." I explained. "I'm glad it happened so close to the park so I could walk home. You know, I really do need to carry a cell phone."

Off she scurried to save the van. I had parked it just around the corner with a stuffed animal on the steering wheel and the sign said it: April Fool!

So it goes year after year. We have been together for nineteen years and I think I have gleefully shouted, "April Fool!" nineteen times. That is nineteen to zero, quite a record in my favor. What is so puzzling to me is that she doesn't even try to get me. It's like she becomes paralyzed with anticipatory fear.

Didn't Sophia learn—like I did—from the masters of merciless plans, Edgar Alan Poe and Alfred Hitchcock? Now, those boys were ruthless. I remember one of Hitchcock's shows in which a paralyzed man realizes that all he can move is one pinkie finger. He is lying on a slab in the morgue and he knows he has to move that pinkie at just the right instant to let someone know that he is alive. At the exact right moment, Hitchcock has a mortician move the man from the slab into the coffin. The paralyzed man ends up lying on that very pinkie. No one is ever going to see him move it! The fact that he is still conscious slowly sinks into the viewer's brain as the clumps of dirt fall onto the coffin. End of show.

"O, that's terrible!" I remember shouting. I was a student nurse at Ypsilanti State Psychiatric Hospital, somewhere near Detroit at the time. We watched the only available television in a poorly lit cement basement. Dark corridors led to the wards of 5,000 under-medicated patients and we could hear heavy metal doors clanging and footsteps. I was scared out of my mind watching Hitchcock down there, but I kept coming back for more.

Stories like that on television and studying authors like Poe in high school gave me this courage to be ruthless. Didn't she do that? I'm sure having an older brother who liked to terrorize me helped, too, but Sophia has an older brother.

What's wrong with her?

Last year, Year Nineteen, she stated decisively that I had crossed a line and that she saw absolutely no humor in my joke. Plus, it wasn't easy to talk her out of being really ticked off for a good long time. I had to agree; my joke back-fired. Here's what happened:

Along with being a nurse, Sophia is a licensed massage therapist. As a client I can vouch for the fact that she is very detailed in her work; she is great at it. All her clients say so. She graduated from a certified massage therapy school in Portland, Maine and is licensed in the state of Maine where she has practiced for a number of years. Arizona also requires licensing for massage therapists and its licensing agency charges a hefty fee for doing so. Because Sophia does not advertise and takes, as clients, only friends who live in our park, she did not get licensed in Arizona. From time to time she worries about someone turning her in to the authorities.

On April 1st of last year my brother and I had driven in to Phoenix for our weekly infusions and Ursula, a fun-loving soul, was our nurse, per usual. It occurred to me to have Ursula pose on the telephone as an inspector for the Professional Licensing of Health Occupations. Ursula was fantastic! Without a moment's hesitation and very professionally, she explained that she was from the licensing agency and that she wanted to check out Sophia's massage practice. She asked to set up an appointment. Sophia curtly responded saying that she didn't know what her schedule was, that she would have to call back and then abruptly hung up. At least that is how Ursula described it to me.

When I attempted to call Sophia a few minutes later to say, April Fool, she didn't answer the phone. After several more unsuccessful attempts to reach her, I became a wee bit concerned so I called and asked my sister-in-law, Joyce, to walk over to our trailer to tell Sophia what the deal really was. Joyce went over, but somehow in the translation of things, did not tell Sophia about the joke.

"She is not answering the phone," Joyce reported back to me, "because she thinks the inspector woman might try to call her again."

A couple of hours later brother and I came home and Sophia was waxing the van in the car port. I stepped out of brother's Chevy Suburban and crowed my usual, "April Fool!"

There was a very long pause. I walked up to Sophia and looked more closely into her face and eyes. Most disturbingly, I saw no indication of sudden enlightenment or even the barest hint of a smile. It was as if she had not heard me.

"Did something go wrong today?" I pressed glibly.

"Yes," she said tersely, "and I am very upset about it. What do you mean, 'April Fool'?"

Oh, boy, this is bad, I thought, and hastened to explain: "It was Ursula; she posed as somebody from the licensing agency. It was a joke. I asked her to pretend. Why didn't you answer the phone right afterwards? I called right back to say April Fool."

Sophia stood. Her jaw dropped. "It was you?" she demanded.

"Yes, it was me!"

"How could you?" she seethed and turned on her heel to go indoors.

That was last year. This year I see a plastic chunk of feces lying in front of the toilet on the bathroom floor and it looks shockingly real. I am not fooled but here in Year Twenty I suddenly have to deal with Sophia's first act of revenge on April 1st. Wow!

What is next? Being tied to the bed in our hot, cramped bedroom, a room of torture like in Poe's *The Pit and the Pendulum*, while a knife—strapped to a blade of the ceiling fan, no doubt—twirls madly above my navel? Should I worry about being buried alive—like Poe buried Fortunato in *The Cask of Amontillado*—under the patio bricks that she put in place this past winter? Maybe she's been plotting something for a whole year; now that I think of it, she actually is quite inscrutable at times and not to reciprocate in nineteen years really isn't normal. I'm not kidding or being sarcastic; I am having some real concerns here. I don't know, for instance, if there is any dissuading of a street smart person once they get locked into revenge. In fact, do I even know what a street smart person is actually all about? There is nothing about them in my textbooks.

From Maine Again

Chapter Nine

In-Laws: Ya Gotta Love Em!

IN-LAWS, WHAT A CHALLENGE! Officially, I am not married but I sure enough, after all these years of living with Sophia, have in-laws—Greek in-laws, no less. They are ever true to their thespian forbearers and each embodies a unique version of the hero's tragic flaw. Sophia and her siblings on almost a daily basis act out a resplendent repertoire of dramas, melodramas and tragic-comedies. Since 1980, when Sophia and I moved from Colorado to Maine, I have done all I can to keep up with the many and varied plots and subplots.

Basil lives alone in a big house on the corner of Ocean Avenue and Webhannet Street—only a short walk from our house. He has a spacious lawn, a fantastic view of the ocean—especially from the third floor balcony and the widow's walk up on the roof—and imported Italian floor tiles. He is a heavy set, tall, forceful Greek man, a divorce and personal injury lawyer, who has two grown sons and who has consorted with an assortment of "pretty girl(s) with (a) great figure(s)...not one (any) of those feminist types" during the almost fifteen years that I have known him.

Basil and I stand eye to eye—if two people can do that while always keeping a minimum of four feet between them. I am fiercely independent, love being a feminist and am more comfortable in relationships with women than men; need I say that he and I have had a rocky relationship? In the past, in fact, he has gone so far as to ostentatiously ostracize me from family gatherings. There were never any explanations as to why they occurred. They just did. He was making an alpha male kind of statement of some kind or other. Sophia would get the invitations but not me. When he was still living with Joy, his wife, that kind of thing didn't happen. She liked me okay, whereas Basil is ambivalent at best. I understand where he is coming from; I feel the same way about him and we have had some pretty interesting ups and downs.

For instance, right after the wedding of his son Michael in the spring of '93, Basil and I were doing great. We even exchanged whole sentences. That is, until I just absolutely had to step out of the Stepford Wife box for a second. Try not to prejudge me; given the circumstances, you might have, too. First I want to tell you about the circumstances that had brought us to that great place and then I'll tell you about my fall from grace.

You see, Basil was in the middle of remodeling his kitchen and was woefully behind in wedding reception preparations—his house to be the wedding reception site—that April when Sophia and I returned from Arizona. There were only three days before the special day, mind you, and backsplash wall tiles still needed grout, electrical wires still protruded from outlet boxes, construction debris was strewn everywhere and floors were tracked with dirt. The new stove, microwave and refrigerator were in huge cardboard boxes nowhere near where they needed to be. All of the dishes and kitchen items along with Basil's briefcase, clean and dirty shirts and suit pants were all stashed in the living room. It was obvious that Basil needed help, and Sophia and I were oh-so-kind to bail him out.

Still fighting jet-lag, I froze my buns and fingers off cleaning long-neglected, caked-on food waste from Basil's filthy old refrigerator. He had moved it into his garage as a backup to his new one. He had tons of food—always a priority for him—coming, he said. As I scraped and scrubbed, dirty brown water dripped from the wrists and elbows of my patched, darned, favorite, old, wool navy sweater. It was a miserable day, as I remember it. Rain was pouring from the top of the garage door not a foot from where I was working and the steel gray ocean was relentlessly pounding its cold waves against the rocks. My nose dripped the entire time. I didn't say that being back in the family fold was necessarily a wonderful thing, did I?

Someday I probably won't remember the chaos or the cold of those few days. And I might not remember the lid of the garbage can sailing towards me through the air as Basil sped off in the loaded pickup truck to go to the dump. Or the brown Christmas tree coming back in the truck because it wasn't the day for wood products at the dump. Hopefully, though, I will remember the MacDonald's double cheeseburger that he pushed into my freezing hands—he should have known that I don't eat those things but as a hand warmer it was pretty good—and the corsage which was just like his sisters' corsages that he provided for me at the reception.

That was sweet—and, no doubt, those will be precious memories someday—but a cheap double cheeseburger and a corsage just weren't enough for me. I had slogged through his stuff for three whole days, all to make him look good, and, in my thinking, he still owed me big time. I, unhealthily, harbored and nursed such thoughts along for a couple of months after the wedding—even though ostensibly we were doing great—and then, all of sudden one day the Stepford-Wife-out-of-the-box-opportunity presented itself. I am not proud of it but, truth be told, I succumbed to greed. You must understand; it's not easy living on a fixed income a few houses away from an affluent relative. Now and then, I just wanted to get my hands on a piece of that wealth; it was just too tempting.

It went like this. Basil had brought home an unassembled grill. It was when he was first dating Patti and he wanted to make a good impression; so, of course, he had bought the Cadillac of barbecue grills. It included the rotisserie, a couple of holding trays and a bunch of other knobs and gadgets.

Coincidentally, a couple of weeks earlier, Sophia and I had assembled our own grill in our living room. It was more along the lines of a subcompact like an Escort, a stripped down, basic, small version of a grill in other words. I am scared of gas and fires and had been freaked out by the whole idea at first. However, having personally handled the burner assembly and having successfully managed to get the venturi springs to fit into both the venturi and the valve—plus attaching the igniter wire to the electrode in the collector box—I had been reassured. It took us the better part of an afternoon.

You will know whereof I speak—if you have lived any length of time at all—when I say that two brains are never wired in the same manner. Consequently, each brain has its own interpretation of instructions—most often poorly written in the first place. This time around Sophia and I had emerged victorious without too much damage having been done to our relationship: a bit of a coup for us, and we were quite proud. Sophia had bragged about it to Basil.

So there we were—Basil, Sophia and I. It was getting late; darkness was gathering and Sophia and I had followed him out to his front driveway.

He said, "They wanted $30.00 at the store to assemble this grill and I thought you might want to make that $30.00. If not, I'll just have them do it. It makes no difference to me. It's up to you. If you don't want to do it, I won't even take it off the truck."

I walked around to the back of the truck and the size of the box amazed me. I started to think: *we'll have to work on this in his garage and it's still darn cold out there. We'll have to bundle up and working will be cumbersome. Not to mention when it is a damp, raw cold like that, I don't breathe very well. I'll have to talk and move around when I'm not breathing very well. I'll get irritable. Sophia will get irritable. Because of the extra attachments, it is going to take us a lot longer to do than ours. I don't relish going through the bickering again not right now when we're so fresh from doing our own.*

And then I heard the two of them talking about dismantling two old broken down grills as well, maybe saving some parts and Sophia offering to take the rest to the dump. Plus, I figured, he was not going to want to take this new one back 25 miles to Portsmouth.

"Fifty dollars," I asserted boldly. Bold, I realized instantly, was an approach I had not previously used with Basil.

Basil looked at me. I was on his left side, his bad ear. He turned to Sophia, "What'd she say?"

"She said $50.00. She's saying we'll assemble it for $50.00." Even on the far side of dusk I could see his eyes harden and his bulky body tense up.

"And a dinner at the Steak House," grinned Sophia, riding the greed gravy train.

He gave us a clipped, "Oh," and a heartless little laugh. Then, directed only to Sophia, he said, "Well, it's up to you. What do you want to do?"

"We'll do it, Basil. Okay, Tjaakje?"

I raised my eyebrows; I knew there was no way out of it; after all, he was doing us a favor, right? I sort of nodded and it was a done deal.

"Did he agree to the $50.00 or to the dinner?" I asked as we walked home in the dark. I was thinking, *Sophia has an inside track and I'm acting like the kid who asks Mom what Dad has decided. I am an adult, for Pete's sake!*

We did it all: the assembly, filled the propane tank, hooked it up, test fired it, called the company to send out the correct instruction booklet, dismantled the other grills, and took them to the dump. Two days later he even brought home two little portable hibachis, one for his car, one for Patti's—he was suddenly into romantic picnics—and we assembled them, too. The check he gave to Sophia in a couple days was made out for $30.00 dollars.

I am not stupid; I know when I have been put in my place. No invitation to join him and new girlfriend at the Steak House either. He'll spend hundreds, thousands regularly. No lie! He buys expensive meals, drinks, jewelry and dresses for his women who are willing to rub their body parts against his and to massage his ego, but he won't give his sister and me the satisfaction of negotiating fairly for $20.00. He takes offense at the very notion. Suffice it to say, I am still working on why I, this avowed feminist, keep falling for all this blatant macho exploitation stuff. It very well might be my tragic flaw. Or would that be my Achilles heel? Are those two one and the same? Whatever.

Sophia, the youngest of the four siblings, and brother Basil have an on-again off-again relationship. They will go for long walks during which Basil reviews his latest love entanglement or disentanglement or some family dilemma with his sons. Sophia will come back from those walks fuming about his morals and not wanting to hear any more of it. "It's always all about him!" she rants. When really fed up, she sends him a letter which is inevitably followed by a protracted hiatus in their get-togethers.

I listen, suggest and advise, knowing full well that it all goes in one ear and out the other. Sophia will say, "But you don't understand; he's my brother!"

On rare occasions they will have what Sophia refers to as "a break through". For instance, not long ago Sophia returned from his house having massaged his pain-filled back and contentedly reported, "Basil and I are cruising along quite well now. We even talked about death yesterday: I said to him, 'When Mother dies, we'll be next and it makes death seem more...' and I couldn't come up with the word. Basil came up with it; he asked, 'Imminent?' and I said, 'Yes, imminent."

Sophia stopped talking at that point and I waited until I couldn't stand it anymore. "Was that it?" I inquired.

"Yeah, that was it," she replied smugly.

Only then did it become clear to me that she was savoring their moment of closeness and did not want me to mess with it. That's one of the things about in-laws: sometimes you're in the loop, sometimes you're not, and you have absolutely no control over what it's going to be or when it's going to change.

Snowbird Stories: Several Degrees Beyond Common Sense

Louise is the oldest of the foursome and is always stressed to the max with her job as an office manager for an accounting firm in California and with her hour-long, five-days a week commute in heavy city traffic. To restore her sanity, she visits the coast, staying with Basil, every summer for two weeks. She is supportive and a dear; she is also a sports nut which I love about her. It gives us something in common to talk about.

Helen, on the other hand, is quite another story and, of course, there is our history with her as well.

After Sophia and I had lived in proximity to Basil for about five years, he saw it as his duty one evening in midsummer to alert the family to his observation that "Sophia hates all men." Philemon, Helen's husband, a Greek Orthodox priest, not to be outdone apparently, then saw it as his duty to call Sophia the next morning to say, "You are living in sin and I will hear your confession." To which Sophia took great umbrage and declined in her inimitable forthright manner. Helen, in turn, as the stand-in presbyter, expounded—for a full 45 minutes without taking a single breath—on sanctification to me. When she ended her last point, I vaguely remember railing back at her something about Biblical things in general and a few specifics about Jesus being tolerant of everyone and not speaking on the issue of same sex alliances. Trust me; it was not a pretty sight.

Helen and I have, since our verbal sanctification skirmish, been more civilized to one another. However, at the slightest provocation we'll still heat up the telephone wires with our sermons on the shoulds of life in these United States. There is no possibility of my cleaning a refrigerator as a sacrificial offering in her case since she lives in Michigan, and I did not get invited to her daughters' weddings on account of "the parishioners, you know;" so any meaningful progress in this relationship of ours has been slow in coming.

Helen and Philemon live in Southgate, a suburb of Detroit, and the two will vacation on the coast of Maine some summers. This is one of the summers that Helen and Philemon are visiting and they are staying over at Basil's house.

Anyway, as the broom of life sweeps me along—at least in regard to my in-laws—Basil, Helen and I—for Sophia's sake—have mellowed in the intervening years. It is 1998—eighteen years into these relationships— and, for the most part now, I am included in the family fold. This inclusion does not mean, however, that we are comfortable in one another's presence. To be entirely truthful, I must say that it is exhausting for me to socialize with these Greek in-law folks. I am always on guard; I still have—as do they, I believe—a good bit of in-law wariness. Which is why, last night, when I was cosmically accorded the opportunity, I took full advantage and soaked up some heavenly moments of superiority over the whole founders-of-Western-civilization, olive-skinned, olive-feta-cheese-eating, Mediterranean lot of them.

The setting was a balmy evening following a humid, hot, testy late July day. It was after the steamed clams, boiled lobster, garden salad, beet greens, corn on the cob, pasta and rolls but before dessert and coffee. I will say on Basil's behalf—and the sisters, too—that he is extremely generous when it comes to food. One never leaves hungry and often gets leftovers to take home. In fact, he could feed the whole neighborhood with his leftovers. After dinner the five of us were gallantly trying to be relaxed in one another's company up on Basil's third floor balcony. Between sparse but pleasant sounding sentences we watched the ocean waves come and go and the tourists walk, bike or go by in trolleys down below on Ocean Avenue. I remember thinking, *if those people were to look up here, they might enviously imagine us to be a typical, well-to-do, carefree, loving American family.* Priceless, the irony, really.

Basil had told a familiar joke. There had been a few polite chuckles, a brief lull and then I said, "Let me tell you about this man who bought himself a new dog that had a reputation for being an excellent birder."

Sophia, with a quick, sharp sound, sucked in her breath. She had not heard this joke and mentally, I figured, she was predicting that it would either be about sex or religion, my favorite topics for jokes—both, obviously, hot buttons for this audience. With false bravado, I thought: *she needs to lighten up; her family members and I have to struggle to get the lifeblood into our wings of friendship in our own way—right?—and she really shouldn't try to orchestrate it.*

Basil, I was pleased to see, cocked his good ear towards me and the orthodox duo leaned forward just a smidge.

"The man," I proceeded, "built his blind out by the lake and waited with his new dog for the ducks."

Being from *away,* as they say here in Maine, I knew from the outset that this was a risky venture—however, worth it, if successful. My joke was a *down home* type of joke which, no doubt, would have been better told by a native, let alone that it did have a religious reference, but, undaunted by the obvious, I pressed on.

"Soon some ducks flew over. He raised his rifle..." and at this point I paused to physically demonstrate the man's actions. I sat erect, extended both arms out in front of me and pointed my forefingers, sighting the ducks over my upraised left thumb near my face (I am left-handed) and moving the rifle in a slow arc with my extended right arm and hand. The deck served as my duck blind and the whole ocean was my lake.

"He trained it on a duck," I continued, "shot, and the duck fell into the water. The dog instantly ran out on top of the water and brought back the duck. Only his pads got wet."

At the mention of the dog running on top of the water, I could see Philemon and Helen become a shade defensive and uneasy, but I could also see, I was holding their interest; in fact, even more so now, they were following every word. The priest rubbed his sunburned forehead; Helen dabbed at her nose with a tissue.

Sophia, at my mention of the walking on water, squirmed and had one of her coughing spells. I paused and smiled—impishly, I presume—at her. Basil belched and tugged at one side of his crotch; when I see him do that, I quickly look away. The man acts like a baseball player with a protective cup, always making adjustments in that department; he has no shame. He had been complaining repeatedly about being uncomfortable from having eaten too much and from the warm humid night. Normally, he would have been shirtless but not in the presence of the priest apparently. He was wearing khaki Bermuda shorts with a white pullover and large flip flop-like sandals on his feet. The back of his pullover and deeply tanned face were wet with sweat. Plus, it was obvious to me that Basil was having trouble being the listener; he so much more prefers to be the teller of the jokes. Helen took a studied sip of water and offered Sophia a glass. Sophia waved it off with one hand and tried to get control of herself.

"The man was stunned," I said when all had settled. "And, sure enough, it happened a second time and then a third. He pondered the situation a good long time and finally decided that he had to have his friend see this dog walk on water to make sure that he wasn't seeing things wrongly."

Sophia rummaged around in her pockets for her lip gloss, solemnly applied it and put her instruction into the form of a question, "Tjaakje, can you wrap this up pretty soon? I am ready for dessert and it's getting late."

"Absolutely," I say in a self-assured manner, remembering to savor every single second.

"Sophia, let her tell the story. Don't interrupt her," admonished Helen, and I was so thrilled to have not only her attention but her support! This was huge! I gave her a big smile and kept going, making sure that I kept my voice elevated so that Basil would not miss a word.

"The man tells his friend about having this new dog and wanting him to see the dog at work. His friend agrees and the two take a day to go to the lake. They sit quietly in the duck blind and wait. A few ducks fly over and the man trains his rifle (me, too, in the demo again) and shoots. The duck falls and the dog runs out on the water to retrieve it. The friend says nothing. Same thing happens and the friend still says nothing."

Helen was completely hooked; her eyes were glued to my face. The priest was hooked, too; I could tell by his alert body language, but he didn't want to show it. He looked everywhere but at me. Actually, that was not unusual; he never wants eye contact with me. I wonder, do the serious priest and the missus have anyone in their lives who tells them jokes?

Basil was still straining to hear or just straining against that massive belly of his—I couldn't tell which—but I went ahead and increased the volume yet another notch. *Someone really should tell this man that he needs hearing aids*, I think. Sophia's lips had become cyanotic from the strain and even in the gathering dusk she looked sort of pale. I knew it was time to wrap it up, to put her out of her misery.

"Finally," I asserted, "the man can't stand it and asks, 'Well, what'd ya think of my dog?'"

"The friend draws in slowly on his pipe and just as slowly blows out the smoke before he drawls, 'He's all right, I guess.'"

I hurried on because Helen started to chuckle, thinking that was the end.

"'But, but,' splutters the man, 'What? Didn't ya see? Didn't ya see it walking on water? What'd ya think of that?'"

"'Ayuh,'" says the friend doing the pipe thing again before continuing, 'Guess he can't swim.'"

"Cute! That's cute. Very cute!" erupted Helen with gales of hearty laughter. "Wasn't that cute, Philemon?" She prodded him with her hand on his arm.

The priest stole a glance at me first then looked quickly over at Basil before he allowed a half smile to show. Basil grunted, heaved himself out of the lounger and announced, "I'm going down to start the coffee."

As I relaxed back into my chair to take in those sweetest of moments, I noticed that Sophia looked much better. Her lips and face were a healthier rose color and she asked in good humor, "Where do you get them from, Teej?"

In-laws, ya gotta love em!

Chapter Ten

A Swift, Sharp Verbal Blow

DICK AND BETTY LIVE A COUPLE HOUSES DOWN from me on Hillside Street, the street at the back of my house, and they don't talk to me anymore. It's my fault—no doubt about it; I said something stupid and I did it deliberately. In my defense, at the outset, I will say that Dick and I had been on a collision course for months and months and I really did try to avoid it. I did. But it was just bound to happen. I knew it, Sophia knew it, but Dick didn't have any idea.

This nemesis of mine had been a shop teacher in Pennsylvania for many years but had to retire because of his bad kidneys. He and Betty moved to southern Maine—where they had previously been vacationing in the summer time—and with Dick's shop skills and tools, he turned a cheap, rundown cottage into a nice house. Betty has all the before-and-after pictures to prove it. Dick loves showing the place off; it is his pride and joy. Fine, I congratulate him. What turned into a problem with me was his insatiable curiosity and inordinate need to act as this self-appointed know-it-all teacher and consultant for every neighborhood building project from a simple replacing of a board in a set of steps to the construction of a whole new house.

This was always the scenario: first, I would hear a Mack truck with its huge Builtmor equipment on a flatbed round the tight corner from Ocean Avenue onto Hillside Street or Highland Avenue heading towards someone's project—the revs, squeals and clunks were all so unmistakable—and immediately thereafter I would hear Dick's screen door banging shut behind him as he hurried to keep up with the flatbed. It wasn't just the trucks, the mere thud of a piece of wood falling on the ground or the whine of a skill saw would bring Dick to your side, too. It was as if he kept his ear to the ground and heard the sounds as they traveled up the granite ledge underneath our homes. I swear, he observed every step of every project within a half mile and every other step within a mile of his place.

In the first year of my living on Hillside Street, I had two dormers enlarged on the second floor and it became commonplace to encounter Dick coming down my staircase when I had not even known that he had come into the house! He would wax on with members of my work crew and I'd see the dollar bills floating off into thin air while he expounded on some irrelevant fact or other.

When I started working on a project of my own, like redoing the pantry shelves, he was there after the first blow of my hammer. He had an annoying laugh about my mistakes and within minutes he would have revised my tentative plan to suit his own vision. If I continued with my scheme, he would say, "No, that's not what I meant." He'd laugh some more, sigh impatiently, reach for the tool I was using, move himself into the field of activity and start showing me what he meant.

To him, I was the addle-headed clumsy high school adolescent he had tried to teach for twenty-seven years. To me, he was the irritable father who didn't think it worth his time to teach me because I was a girl.

I remember it like it was yesterday. When I was six and my brother, John, was eight we still had to do the dishes together. He would dry and I would wash. While I put dish soap in the basin, ran the hot water, gathered the silverware, dropped it into the basin to soak and started to wash the glassware, he was supposed to clear and wipe the table. Glassware finished, I moved on to coffee cups and saucers. Table cleared, John moved on to plowing a field. He pretended that his hand was the tractor and the dishrag the plow. The crumbs were the furrow he was plowing, and with each complete walk around the table, the crumbs inched closer to the center of the table. He putt-putted like a John Deere tractor around the table until my dish rack could hold no more. I either had to dry the dishes or call this situation to the attention of my mother. Like a loyal employee concerned about company success, I informed management and expected quick reprisal.

Wrong. Logic did not apply. There was a whole other world revolving out there of which hitherto I had been blessedly oblivious. Darn it anyway, why does our consciousness have to expand?

Instead of a reprimand, my mother said, "Isn't he cute? It is the way boys are. He is pretending. Soon, he won't want to do dishes at all."

Sure enough, soon, he didn't want to do the dishes, and guess who didn't make him, and guess who wasn't given a choice about having to keep doing them, and guess who was washing not only the dishes but also the woodwork, the linoleum and polishing a bunch of shoes every Saturday while brother breathed the wonderfully scented farm air, sloshed in rain puddles and pounded nails into fresh wood?

You'd think Dick could have sniffed danger in the air around me but he didn't, like Dad didn't and Mom didn't. According to the Bible, Saint Paul said it, "Woman, be inferior to the man." That was the prevailing principle in our house. What horse manure! I simply wouldn't hear of it. Little mattered more to me after that than getting on the road to becoming free and equal.

Dr. Aycrigg, hospital administrator, my boss, paid me a huge compliment one day. He said, "I don't like it when you say I'm a chauvinist but I listen because I have three daughters and I owe it to them to learn what they're up against in this society." Bless his unique and wonderful male heart! In that moment my fight for equality was affirmed and honored. Why couldn't Dick who had four daughters and no sons have that kind of attitude?

The constant threat of Dick's presence shaped my behaviors. When I wanted to work on my projects, I'd look to see if Dick's car was gone and, if not, I would turn up my music in hopes that he wouldn't hear me. I planned it so that I would work on my projects on the days he went to his dialysis, and, when he did appear at the perimeter of my projects, I made excuses about how I was not going to work on it anymore that day. My patience stretched thin; it was to the point of breaking. I was like a polar bear waiting at an ice hole for a seal to surface. It was inevitable that one time Dick's nose would show up and I'd whack it with my paw into kingdom come.

One day I was on a ladder replacing an old window pane. I had the glass in place and was trying to get the new putty around it to look half-way decent. It was a dirty painstaking job on a hot, humid day—made none the more attractive by the fact that I had broken the original pane with a wayward blow of my hammer. The ear-splitting, pride-shattering sound, of course, had echoed throughout the neighborhood. Anyway, I was up on the ladder and Dick hurried over to supervise, like always.

He planted himself at the foot of my ladder and started in on me. "Juk, juk, juk, he, he, he," went Dick with that jeering laugh of his, and then he said, "So you broke the window. How did you manage that? Juk, juk, juk."

With all the force of a starving bear after a too-long wait on the ice, I struck a swift, sharp verbal blow and retorted, "I fixed it! Forget that I broke it. I've fixed it! You're such a jerk, you know that?"

That did it. Dick scurried away and relations have been strained ever since. He comes over to talk with Sophia in her garden and he and I will say hello when we meet on the street but that's it. There's no denying it; I've enjoyed his absence. I love figuring out the projects for myself, but now I regret hurting him the way I did.

There has been lots of activity over at Dick's house this past week and last night there was quite a party. All of the daughters, spouses and grandchildren are squeezed into that small home for one last hurrah. The moving vans have left and this, I understand, is Dick and Betty's last day in the neighborhood. Dick's health has nose-dived and they are moving to Connecticut so Betty will be near one of the daughters when Dick's time comes.

Apparently, the rest of the clan was sleeping off the party—Dick never drank alcohol; his kidneys couldn't handle it—because, when I was down on one knee cleaning out the cat's litter box and looking out the window over to Dick's house at about 7 a.m., he was all alone. There in his sun-drenched porch, which he enclosed just two years ago and which he and Betty have so enjoyed, he was sitting on a cardboard box with his hands clasped on top of the newspaper in his lap. *An unusual pose for Dick*, I thought. I saw his chest heave several times as he reached into his back pocket for his handkerchief.

Private though it should have been, I was quite transfixed by the unfolding scenario, and I just couldn't pull my eyes away. He held the large handkerchief to his eyes as he took several more large gulps, then wiped his eyes and forcefully blew his nose. Dick was crying.

In that moment I felt my stab of regret. Dick had meant no harm; at least I don't think so. He was lonely and missed the kids he used to teach. We have those things in common, in fact. I miss the students, too. Why couldn't I just have put my arm around the old coot and said, "Dick, I appreciate your suggestions and I love you but I just have to work these things out by myself," and walked him away from my projects. Men love to be coddled like that; I have seen so many women do it. I just don't have the instincts for it and today my deficiency in that department really saddens me.

Even if I couldn't do that, I could have gone over to Dick today, apologized and wished him well but I didn't do that either. A polar bear wouldn't do that for a seal, but as one human to another, I should have. Shame on me. In sadness and reflection, after Dick and Betty and their clan had left, it came to me: I have been too fiercely focused on being independent. So much so, in fact, that compassion and common decency in me have gone by the wayside. From now on and for Dick's sake, I will expect better of myself.

Chapter Eleven

Some New Wrinkles in the Routine

IT HAS BEEN TEN YEARS—since January of 1990—that I have been getting the weekly intravenous infusions. One day a week I travel to a facility, get a needle inserted in a vein in my arm and sit for an hour in a recliner while receiving the plasma product. In Mesa, John and I have to handle eight-lane heavy traffic to go into the heart of Phoenix to the doctor's office. In Maine, at a much slower pace, I go south from Wells on Route One—through Ogunquit, past the Ogunquit Summer Playhouse where recently we shook hands with MASH's Hot Lips Hoolihan, the real Loretta Swit, past Flo's, which is a popular hotdog stand in a rundown old shack with a cantankerous, old gray-haired woman in a hairnet serving her delicious secret sauce on steamed hotdogs, and turn east off Route One into York Village—to small York Hospital. The leaves of the maple, birch and oak trees are turning their brilliant autumn colors now and so it was a lovely ride today.

Sometimes, though I didn't today, I'll have lunch with my friend, Ginnie, in the hospital cafeteria. She is a volunteer with Hospice as was I a couple of years ago. (I was a grief support group facilitator.)

Because of my connection with Hospice and even though I was not considered "terminal," which is—under normal circumstances—a requirement for reimbursement, the director assigned me two volunteers, Jennie and Ginny, when I was getting my chemotherapy. As I weakened from low blood counts back then, Jennie or Ginny would drive me to treatments and sit with me. What a tremendous help and support they were! Both women live in York. Jennie works in the thrift shop and we chat when I donate something. Her husband, Jerry, is a plumber and he installed the toilet in my new downstairs bathroom for nothing. They are wonderfully caring and generous people.

Ginny and I like to sit and talk about our relationships, ourselves, movies and books. She is a friend who always gives me a new and important perspective One such day, for example, I shared with her my lofty goal of wanting to die in the way Scot Nearing, the author and political radical, had. When he reached his 100th birthday, he began voluntarily fasting and died peacefully at home never having gone to a hospital or a doctor. I also told Ginny that I was reading Helen Nearing's book, <u>Light on Aging and Death</u>. Ginny, being infinitely more practical, replied simply, "I just want to die without pins in my underwear and no hair on my legs!"

Anyway, I want you to know in advance that I am very fond of Hospice, the hospital, and its volunteers. Usually, I have my infusion and then drive myself back home. Not a big deal.

This week, however, after I had walked through the hospital entranceway with its two sets of double doors, I could see that there was to be a new wrinkle in my usual routine. A rather large desk and a rather short, white-haired volunteer, stationed to one side of it, were effectively blocking the hallway to the elevators. The diminutive, dutiful pink lady asked me where I was going. *Given all the privacy laws, I should tell her that it is really none of her business*, I thought, but I pleasantly told her anyway. She insisted that I first had to check in at the Admissions Office.

"I come regularly," I replied confidently and politely. "Arrangements have been made so that I don't have to stop in at Admissions every week." As if stone deaf, she said, "Everyone goes. You must. It is right down this hallway." She started in that direction expecting me to follow, which gave me just enough time to get by the desk.

"I don't have to go there," I retorted—a bit clipped this time, I will admit—and proceeded towards the elevators instead.

The overly zealous, pink-clad little dictator quickly changed course and stepped in front of me. She declared firmly, "I am only trying to save you a trip back down here."

"Thanks, I do appreciate that," I smiled thinly and stepped around her.

Luckily, one elevator door was open so I darted inside. Undaunted, the pink person put her hand on the door and held it back. I pushed the button again and the door pushed against her hand. We repeated these actions twice more, both outwardly appearing to still be handling this quite civilly, and then with a loud exasperated sigh, she turned on her heel and went back to her desk.

When I finished my treatment, a new pink lady offered to escort me out. This was not the standard protocol since I do not require a wheelchair; but knowing how hospitals operate, I didn't mind. *This may be*, I rationalized, *the first day on the job for a new batch of volunteers.*

As we walked down the hallway, the new lady asked, "What will I say I am doing with you?"

I sorted the question through for a short while and then queried, "Who is going to ask or whom do you have to tell?"

"We have to write down what we do. I can't say that I am discharging you." She looked troubled and I was empathetic; unlike the feisty little chipmunk coming in, this one seemed like the fragile type.

"How about saying that you're walking with me?" I suggested lightly.

"We don't do that," she replied decisively.

"Um hum," I murmured.

We walked in silence for a ways, each puzzling over her dilemma and then entered the elevator.

"Would escorting me work?" I asked.

When the door opened, I breathed a sigh of relief to see that my former nemesis had left her post. My new pink challenge walked on ahead of me several paces and then stopped to look back to see where I was.

"I can't walk that fast," I informed her somewhat breathlessly.

"I think I won't say anything about you," she said.

"That's fine with me," I responded, a little hurt but understanding.

I could tell that she was pondering it some more as we made our way towards the exit.

"I think that will be okay. I just won't say I did this. Here's the door," she said abruptly and turned to leave.

As I walked slowly towards my car, I fussed aloud, "Who are these people?" It had been cool inside and I was happy to be out in the sun again.

Basking in the warmth of my car, I sat and reflected for a couple of minutes before starting the engine. I shook my head and chuckled. *All volunteers have to start sometime;* I thought, *they don't just show up and become a Jennie or Ginny overnight. Plus, some days, I guess, are just meant to be more interesting than others. If it weren't that way, I'd probably just die of outright boredom from all the monotonous repetition of this disease business. And face it, Teej, that would not be a good thing.*

Nonetheless, I was happy on the way home that Flo's hotdog with the secret sauce was exactly the same and as mouthwateringly delicious as always.

Chapter Twelve

Mrs. Firth Lies in Repose

HAD I KNOWN HOW THE VIEWING OF THE BODY would unfold and what I would see when I leaned down to look into the coffin, I would have borrowed a better camera, one that would take close-ups and show details even in poor lighting. As it was, I had only my cheap Instamatic. It was inadequate and so I have no proof of what I saw. I can offer you, however, my integrity as a guarantee that what I am about to tell you is a God's-honest-truth true story. That, by the way, is really quite a substantial guarantee because those who know me know that I can only tell a lie on April Fool's Day and this is autumn, not anywhere near April 1st.

A little background for you who may still doubt me is that back in the forties and fifties—when right and wrong were not yet shades of gray—my parents taught me to take each of the Ten Commandments literally. "Thou shalt not bear false witness" in my young mind, therefore, came to have the same weight as "Thou shalt not kill". If I broke either commandment, I would at my death go to hell; it was that simple. So, lying and killing are not things I do.

For your full appreciation of the circumstances in which I found myself last evening—and why I should have used a better camera—it would be best to begin at the beginning. Allow me to introduce you to my neighbors: the living Al and Gertrude Ronco and the late Richard Ronco and Mrs. Firth.

Al and Gertrude live directly across the narrow street from the back of my house. Their glassed-in front porch faces my glassed-in back porch. When looking over at them, one sees that a half of their porch is unusable because of years of discarded items which reach all the way up to the ceiling. An attempt to hide this unseemly accumulation with pull-down shades was long ago foiled by damaging sun rays in summers and moisture from frozen windows in winters. Several of the yellowed, stained shades are torn and their lifeless tatters are held up in odd configurations by discarded, dusty items pressing them against the glass of the windows.

An old, once rose-colored curtain separates that half from the remainder of the porch, and there, too, in the middle is the doorway to the house. On that other half of the porch reside five, mismatched, plastic and aluminum, folding lawn chairs. They face outward towards my porch. The entranceway to the porch from outdoors is around that side. The bricks in the steps from the pavement of the street to a small landing and in more steps up to the entranceway are dangerously uneven. These are all to my right as I face them and on the opposite side of where their car is parked. That is to my left and down a rather steep hill. Consequently, when the Roncos come and go, I watch from my porch or from the window above my kitchen sink with more than a little trepidation.

Richard, the only offspring of Al and Gertrude—and, by all accounts, an early bloomer and rising star in the field of education in Wells—died four years ago at the age of thirty-one. The young man, who gave his older parents so much joy and pride, died in Al's arms in the old armchair in the living room. He'd had one of cancer's more horrific deaths, esophageal cancer. The traumatic ordeal and loss stunned this small family into a way of life that now centers on preserving their memories of him.

Mrs. Firth was Gertrude's mother and lived with the couple for all of their forty years of marriage. She was ninety-one when she passed recently. Al is said to have had a previous marriage and I understand he has two daughters from that marriage but I've never seen either; I don't know that they come to visit. Al, in his early 80s, is 20 years older than Gertrude. He actually was closer in age to Mrs. Firth than he is to Gertrude.

Al has the shortening and the stoop in his spine of osteoporosis, and he has the imbalance of twisted feet. He wears dark clothing: usually a pair of dark brown polyester pants that have lots of snags in the thighs, a small assortment of short-sleeved pullovers and a grimy, navy baseball cap in summer, a much-used navy sports jacket and black stocking hat in winter and heavy twisted black shoes. He is very thin, a bit unkempt, his sun-damaged hands shake a lot, he is hard of hearing, he has a stubborn tired-tightness in his otherwise kind, weather-wrinkled face and he sounds like an authentic old—Downeaster which he is.

Al is my Mr. Bo Jangles. In the mornings he totters in place on the pavement of the street, looks to see if I am watching from my kitchen window and, if so, he pantomime's the day's temperature with a hand across the brow, a tighter wrap of the jacket or a shivering self-hug. We always wave and smile at one another; I like him a lot.

Not that long before her passing, Mrs. Firth, hardly an inch over four feet, if at all, quite overweight and quite doughy, still was able to participate in a family ritual. Each and every day—rain, sleet, snow or shine—I would watch as Al helped his aged mother-in-law into the back of the four-door, maroon Buick sedan. He would push at parts of her body while Gertrude stood by and snapped out instructions and admonitions.

Gertrude has a brittle disposition; she always has a hard expression on her face and her words and movements are abrupt and sharp. Her tightly permed, medium-length curls are dyed pitch-black, which puts them in stark contrast to her spindly, buttermilk white legs, white anklets and white nursing-type shoes that are cracking from the multiple layers of white shoe polish. She doesn't care about fashion but she does care about being neat and proper. I got the impression though, as I watched the threesome on a daily basis, that things were getting away from Gertrude a bit— her gray hair roots were showing somewhat more, her slip often showed and she seemed even more frustrated and irritable than normal.

With Mrs. Firth finally in place in the car, Gertrude would get into the front passenger seat and Al—in good weather seasons—would select the day's best flowering plant from his accumulation of flowerpots by the basement entranceway. He would put it into the trunk of the car and off they would go.

When I first moved into the area, other neighbors had been quick to inform me that this curious late-morning excursion always ended up in the cemetery at the gravesite of Richard. What? Had someone actually tailed them one day to learn where they went? Knowing these neighbors, the answer would be: Yes, they had. And, they said, the daily excursion had been going on for four years. Additionally, I had learned, Al makes a personal pilgrimage to his son's grave every morning at 6:30 a.m. I am familiar with it. He revs up the Buick and like a cock's crow at sunrise, I awaken to the noise. From my upstairs window in the predawn light on my way to the bathroom, I see him lighting his cigarette with his shaking hands.

When we chat, Al looks me in the eye and says, "There ain't a day goes by but that I don't get choked up over it. Mor'n Gertrude even."

"Every day?" I ask, trying to fathom the immensity of his unabated grief.

"Ayuh, every day," he says nodding solemnly. "I miss him every day." The ever-present yellowish matter in the innermost corners of his eyes is washed away by the tears that flow freely; from his pants pocket he digs out his none-too-clean, large grayish handkerchief, blows his nose and forgets the ashes on his cigarette which is in his other hand. They drop onto his jacket and he rubs them away.

The high school gymnasium is dedicated to Richard and Al still goes to all the basketball games; like he did when father and son went together. I know because I went with him once. "Usually," he said, "I sit alone." Pictures, various written accolades and sports memorabilia are displayed in a shrine to Richard in their crowded living room.

As time wore on this hot summer, I watched Mrs. Firth slowly but surely lose her strength and the day inevitably came when it was no longer possible to lift, push, pull and roll Mrs. Firth into the Buick. Instead she was left to sit on the back porch while Al and Gertrude made the run to the cemetery. In a few weeks she became weaker and needed help to get to that chair on the porch, just as she had needed help to get into the car. Al told me that she had fallen several times and he was having trouble getting her up. With Gertude's bad back and all, he said, he didn't know how he could keep her going.

Each day, many times over, I waved to Mrs. Firth on the porch. She would wave when I came out of my back door and she would wave when I came around the corner of the house with my laundry basket and again with the garden rake. Sometimes she would add a "Hello" to her wave.

One day, I was in the garden picking green beans and heard Mrs. Firth call, "Hello."

I was occupied. I had to use great caution when moving forward so as not to trample any of Sophia's overlapping vegetables. I was bent downward from the waist to hold each plant with one hand and pick the beans with the other, all the while trying to keep the receptacle for the beans within reach. So, without looking up I called back, "Hello."

I knew Al and Gertrude had gone and that Mrs. Firth was on the porch alone. Again, I heard her call, "Hello. Helloooo."

I figured she must not have heard me the first time and called back more loudly, "Hello. Helloooo."

My basket was half-filled with beans as we echoed our greetings back and forth, each hello a little longer like we were in some thick jungle trying to find our way to one another. I straightened up to ease the strain on my back and to look over at Mrs. Firth. But, much to my surprise, there was no Mrs. Firth to see. Puzzled, I decided to investigate. Mrs. Firth had slipped all the way out of her chair onto the floor. She must have squirmed her way over to the door because that is where she laid flat on her back, calling out, "Helpppp!"

Is it my fault that I have trouble with Maine accents? Wouldn't it be easy for anyone *from away*—as they always call us folks who weren't born in Maine no matter how many years we've lived here—to have heard "hello" in place of "help"? Anyway, with tremendous effort and Mrs. Firth being good-natured about it all, Sophia and I were able to pull her soft body back across the floor and back up into the chair. She was surprisingly heavy and even with the two of us it was not an easy task. I frankly then could not imagine how thin, wobbly Al managed to do so by himself.

Before much more time went by—a week or two at the most—Mrs. Firth was in a hospital bed in the dining room and Al and Gertrude were working hard to keep her alive. Never was she allowed just to lie in bed. Each day a valiant effort was made by the intrepid twosome to get her into the old armchair and to have her walk a few steps. Gertrude would get disgusted because she thought Mrs. Firth wasn't trying to use her legs anymore.

She would rebuke her loudly, "Mother, you are not helping! You'll get too weak. You must try!"

At last, Mrs. Firth slept through the times of getting up. She wouldn't open her eyes nor move a muscle. One day falling backwards, Al landed in the chair with Mrs. Firth on top of him. He told me that same day that he was lucky to have gotten out of it alive. He said that meant he wasn't going to do it again, no matter what Gertrude wanted or said.

Soon after, in spite of their very best efforts, Mrs. Firth died. Another dreaded death in the family and poor Gertrude had to face all those energy-draining arrangements again; at least she knew what was needed this time.

"Would you take pictures for me?" she asked when I was over there to express my condolences.

"Sure," I said a bit too hurriedly which naturally necessitated me having to ask a while later, "Of what exactly do you want pictures?"

"Of Mother," snapped Gertrude, "of Mother at the viewing."

Okay, then. *Will there never come an end to my wanting to be accepted by the locals*? I chided myself crossing the street back to my porch. *Had I even intended to go to this viewing*? Sigh.

Regardless, there I was a few days later, arriving at the funeral home with my little Kodak Instamatic. I entered the room where Al, Gertrude and funeral home staff member stood in dimmed lighting. The open coffin was at the front of the room. Immediately upon seeing me, Gertrude grabbed my upper arm and pulled me off to the side. Such unusual behavior! I had tried to hug her once but she had become startlingly rigid in my embrace. After that mutual embarrassment, we hadn't touched. Actually all of my interactions with Gertrude were a bit prickly and, not to toot my own horn, but I'm pretty sure it wasn't about me. I've never seen her touch or be touched by anyone and she is pretty snippy with everybody.

"A terrible upsettin' thing's happened!" she hissed into my ear, the whole while keeping her tight hold on my arm.

Obviously, I noted internally, *whatever this crisis is, it has taken precedence over her aversion to touch. Ouch*!

Gertrude, unmindful of the fact that she was hurting me and that a couple had now entered the room, blurted out the whole scenario to me.

"A few weeks before Mother's death," she wheezed, "Mother asked me to search the closet for her new, blue dress. I knew there was no new blue dress in any closet, but I didn't argue."

Gertrude said she had searched up and down in every closet and then—after several more times of fake searching—had finally convinced Mrs. Firth to forget about the dress. However, when Mrs. Firth died, Gertrude remembered the blue dress conversations.

 "So I took it to mean that Mother wanted to be buried in a new, blue dress."

Gertrude said she had shopped at both Fox Run and Newington Malls in Portsmouth, New Hampshire for just the right dress, but had come away empty-handed. On her way home and at the point of collapse, she thought of the boutique in Ogunquit and decided she could make one last stop. There it was: a beautiful, yet simple, true-blue evening gown. It was much too long and too snug for Mrs. Firth's short, compressed body but Gertrude deduced that no one would know. The gown could be wrapped around her feet in the casket—because the body would be covered from the waist down—and it could stay unzipped in the back. After all, the top front of the gown, the part that would be visible, was lovely; it had long sleeves of fine blue chiffon, a nice scoop neckline and a pattern of sweeping blue stitching through the solid silk fabric of the bodice. Tremendously relieved and grateful that she had accomplished her mission, Gertrude purchased the gown, drove directly to the funeral home and handed it to the funeral director.

"The next day," Gertrude gasped, "I went to the funeral home in the early afternoon and I was shocked to see Mother's milk-white arms through the sheer long sleeves of the gown!"

She realized, she said, that in all the years she could remember, Mother had never had her arms exposed and they looked so cold lying there like that in the casket. Mrs. Firth, Gertrude told me, did not consider it decent to have bare arms and no matter what the temperature, had always worn an undershirt. "I knew I couldn't let her go being cold like that," she declared with firm lips.

Gertrude released my arm at this point but continued talking, despite the fact that several more people had arrived and were looking our way for a signal that they could come and express their condolences. Gertrude, oblivious to any looks, said that the funeral director's wife had found a pink undershirt and together Gertrude and this woman removed the blue gown from Mrs. Firth, put on the undershirt and then replaced the dress. However, upon viewing the finished product, the two had agreed that the pink and blue was too strange a mixture of colors and it really took away from the loveliness of the gown.

Near panic and with time running out before the evening's public viewing, Gertrude hastened to The Globe, the local discount store, in Wells. It was almost time for closing. The salesgirl heard Gertrude's request for a light blue or white long-sleeved undershirt but was unable to find the exact item. She sorted through various garments that might suit the need and came up with a long-sleeved white T-shirt that had a tiny blue pattern in it.

Gertrude saw the shirt and instantly decided that it would be perfect. "I thought the blue figure might even be attractive under the plain see-through blue of the long sleeves. I dropped the shirt off at the funeral home and had to hurry home to dress and get back here for this."

It may all have been my imagination but I believe Gertrude wanted to look her best—she had on a nice belted, navy blue dress with white collar and white cuffs on short sleeves, black patent leather pumps, some lipstick and her hair nicely combed. She had even found time to have her roots touched up. Al, too, looked clean and pressed. He was wearing a dark brown suit, white shirt and tie—because she wanted to show everyone how well she was handling this second death in the family. She was not proud of how unglued and zombie-like shocked she had been at the events surrounding Richard's burial and she was determined to show her friends and acquaintances that she was made of sterner stuff, that she could perform as well as the next woman under similar circumstances. That was my impression.

At any rate, it was clear as day to me that unless she wrapped up this story soon, she would again leave a less-than-favorable impression. More people were entering the room and first, one and then two had interrupted her story to me as they expressed their sadness over her loss; she had perfunctorily thanked them for their concern and urged them to sign the quest book. Everyone remarked at how well Mrs. Firth looked and at the beauty of the large collection of flowers. From a distance I agreed that Mrs. Firth looked very good; I had never seen her look anywhere near as good. There she was elegantly lying in repose in her evening gown.

At this point Gertrude became distracted and kept watching the people and listening to their remarks as they approached the casket. She herself stayed a good ten feet away, as did Al who wasn't saying much of anything to anybody. During these brief interludes, I tried to imagine what it must have been like to take off the gown repeatedly and to take off and put on the undershirts. The body could not have been in rigor because that would have made it an impossible task. Had it been completely flaccid? I decided that would not have been easy either.

Very careful now not to be overheard, Gertrude continued with her story in hushed, urgent tones. "When I came back to the funeral home tonight, the funeral director's wife showed me the horrible mistake but it was too late to do anything about it!"

Now we were at last getting to the crux of the matter. "What, what horrible mistake?" I asked, barely able to stand the suspense midst the hand shaking and the murmurings of the mourners. She grabbed my arm anew and pulled me over to the casket.

"Don't make it obvious," she spurted, "but look; if you look close, you can see that the little blue figures are bunnies!"

I leaned into the casket smelling the sweet fragrance of formaldehyde and, sure enough, Mrs. Firth, with a restful, amused look on her face, was sporting bunnies on her arms. Plus, to my utter amazement, they were not just the blue outlines of plain, innocent little Easter bunnies; they were the icon of the world-famous Playboy Bunnies!

When I straightened, I saw that Gertrude had moved back to her safe distance of ten feet and was smiling woodenly at the well-wishers. *Mrs. Firth's smile seems so much more genuine than that of her daughter*, I thought unkindly. I drifted back to where she stood.

"I'm so embarrassed," she gushed forth. "Do you think people are noticing? What will I say? What must they think? I'm so embarrassed; what must I do?"

I took a deep breath and then advised her to do the following: "First of all, I don't think people are noticing; nobody is looking that closely. Second of all, if by chance someone did notice and said something, I think you should just laugh. Laugh a little bit, Gertrude, that's what you could do. What else could you do? It really is a funny moment; make a joke of it.

Gertrude's disapproval became evident; she stiffened and scowled. "I think it would be best if you could just laugh," I reiterated. She then huffed aloud at my impertinence and moved away, leaving such a distinct chill in her wake that it made me shiver.

Laugh, love, live, dance, I wanted to shout. ***Come on Mr. Bo Jangles, dance; dance with me!*** Totally inappropriate, I know, but I so loved this stranger-than-fiction scenario; I wanted to share the perfection of it with a kindred soul. I cannot imagine that Gertrude even knows about the Playboy Bunny thing. If she did—no doubt about it—she would be sitting in sack-cloth and ashes begging her late, modest mother's forgiveness forever into eternity.

    I took the pictures and, darn it all, no bunnies showed up, Playboy or otherwise, in any of them. So, you just have to take my word for it. If you do, then you are a kindred soul and it is entirely possible that you and I will dance together some day. I shall look forward to it.

And from Arizona Again

Chapter Thirteen

I'm a Junky and I Have Mrs. Simon Cole to Blame

SOPHIA IS AWAY; she is in Southgate, Michigan, helping her sister, Helen. Helen fractured her tibia when she slipped on a couple of grapes in the cafeteria of Rivergate Terrace, the new nursing home where Mummer lives. Sophia's absence means that I have been left to my own devices and vices for the last two weeks. At first I was enthused; now I am besmirched.

It is Sunday and I have just finished watching—in sequence and nonstop—two National Football League playoff games and a Phoenix Suns National Basketball Association game. My head is filled with "phooizzie", as Sophia would say. That means I have noises in my head from the hours and hours of listening to announcers, commercials and crowd noise. I assure you at the outset; I am not a lazy person—I sew, knit, pay bills and such while I watch—but I will confess: I am hooked, habituated, drunk, stoned and what not all. I am an addict. I infuse—better known as mainline to us hardcore types—inhale and snort sports on television on Sunday.

In the order of things, now that the games are over and the ambiance is peaceful and quiet once again, I have this annoying and familiar sense of having been sullied by my binge; damp, grey clouds of guilt and shame settle into my being, my soul. And, as unlikely as it would seem on the surface, I swear that I have the elderly, now deceased, Mrs.

Simon Cole to blame for this uncontrolled, self-indulgent behavior of mine.

Mrs. Cole and I belonged to the same Dutch community in the Gallatin Valley of southwestern Montana. I never spoke to her directly that I remember, nor she to me, but I knew of her from observation and from eavesdropping on conversations that my mother had about her. Martha Cole was a very short, stout woman who walked with an exaggerated limp—a hip defect from birth, I believe. Yet, from all appearances she was completely undeterred by this lifelong handicap. She had an assertive forthright demeanor, a deep voice, was friendly and outgoing. Her facial features resembled those of Eleanor Roosevelt and like Eleanor, it seemed to me, Martha set the tone in her circles and got things done. There was no doubt in my mind but that she was the undisputed matriarch of the Cole family.

Mrs. Cole and her husband, Simon, who was semi-retired, lived in a home next to their farm. The sons and grandsons now ran the farm. There was a sharp bend in the road right there known as Cole's Corner. It was a half-way point between Churchill, the hub of the Dutch community, and Manhattan, the *American* town. Our farm was near Manhattan; we were sharecroppers. Note: landowners, sharecroppers—huge difference. Martha outlived Simon and in her later years went to live in an efficiency apartment in the Churchill Retirement Home.

This is how the social structure of the community seemed to me in those days: The Alberdas, Boses, Coles, Kimns and Weidenaars were in the upper echelon. These families were, for the most part, settled families who had lived in the community for two or three generations and who had amassed some property and wealth. Then there was the middle tier the Danhofs, the Dyks, Van Dykes and Van Dykens, the Kamps, Emmelkamps and Veltkamps and so forth. Those in the bottom tier were us more recent postwar immigrants from Holland and folks who worked for others or who had not fared so well in the farming business.

It had been common for the upper echelon groups in their pioneering days to have large families and these offspring had also acquired farms and families of their own. A number of these grand- children or great-grandchildren were my classmates in the parochial Christian school. One such was Howard Cole, who happened to be terrific at sports. Those were such vulnerable days for me because I had a crush on Howard and Howard would never so much as cast a sideward glance in my direction. The upper echelon kids and some in the middle tier gave nickel treats to each class member on their birthdays; the rest of us, if we could afford to do so at all, gave penny treats.

In each of the upper echelon groupings there was a respected elder couple. Simon and Martha Cole were one of these couples. It was they who promulgated the mores of the families, and one could observe—as I did, especially after church services when the congregation milled about on the grass and sidewalks and chatted with one another—that they continued to do this promulgating from their retired status. It was also evident that the next generations proudly—and sometimes snootily, I might add—carried the mores forward.

The able men of the families always made up the majority of the elders and deacons in the church consistory, the governing body of the Christian Reformed Church, which was the only kind of church in the community. They also comprised the majority in the Christian School board and from these positions enforced strict Calvinistic religious codes. The women, by example and by giving or withholding praise, set the tone for proper communications and dress code: navy blue with white trim and white gloves for Easter services, after the age of thirteen no hem above the knee, sensible heels—no stilettos—purse hanging from forearm, leave noisy children at home, sit closely next to husband in church, boy next to husband, girl next to mother, no jokes by the preacher, no laughing by the congregation and whispering only if absolutely necessary. Never any swear words and no swear word equivalents. That meant no heck, darn, golly gee whiz or oh my goodness. The demeanor, behavior and attitudes of the Alberdas, Boses, Coles, Kimns and Weidenaars crept into every aspect of our lives. Our family—and I imagine most other families—emulated everything about them—and what we imagined about them since we didn't get invited into their homes.

Being of stoic, northern European roots, our family kept our emotions in, our heads up and our voices down. We especially did so on Sunday, the day that we rested as God had done. We assumed, the Alberdas, Boses, Coles, Kimns, and Weidenaars did the same. On Sunday we attended two one-and-a-half hour church services—the first at nine-thirty in the morning the second at seven in the evening. We younger ones went to catechism after the morning service and the young adults went to Young People's Society after the evening service. After the morning service, we went to the home of family friends—within our appropriate echelon—for coffee and a pastry. Next at home the noon dinner was roast beef, baked potatoes—the heavenly aroma from the oven always wafting tantalizingly towards us as we opened the porch door, thanks to automatic time settings on our new electric stove—green beans and applesauce. After which it was time for an early afternoon nap or reading of church library books. That was followed by tea and a cookie, a few essential chores—such as milk the cows, feed the pigs and chickens, and gather the eggs—a light supper of a boiled egg, a rusk—more commonly known as a zwieback—and a small dish of canned peaches, apricots or pears. It was always the same and no playing of sports, no watching of movies or videos, no television, no rough housing, no card playing and only KGVW, the Christian station, on the radio. This type of Sunday was the model that I carried out into the world with me when I left home to go to Calvin College in Grand Rapids, Michigan to become a nurse.

From early on I was a fan of most all sports—I embroidered all the names of the American and National League baseball teams on my pillowcases—and I was an ardent Yankees fan in those days. While washing down the woodwork in the kitchen and scrubbing the floor on Saturdays, I listened to the Game of the Week with Mel Allen and Dizzy Dean Gillespie; they told me all about Casey Stengel, Whitey Ford, Roger Maris, Mickey Mantle and Yogi Berra. I became a lifelong devotee of Notre Dame Football, too, from their broadcasts on Mutual Radio. Every year I listened to the entirety of the Indianapolis 500 on Memorial Day and every week I listened to the great voice of Don Dunphy on the Gillette Friday Night Fights. Because of him, I loved Rocky Marciano and Sugar Ray Robinson and was crushed in 1952 when Sugar Ray was defeated because of heat stroke in the fourteenth round.

Being a fan of these sports sustained me and I violated no codes in listening to them because they were not on Sunday. I knew that there were professional football games broadcast on television on

Sundays, but I caught the results of the games on Mondays. I was not going to sacrifice my trip to heaven along with the Alberdas, Boses, Coles, Kimns and Weidenaars for a silly old ball game. No sir. I would not crumble. Not me. For four or five years, giving myself over to loftier ambitions, I never once yielded to the ever-pressing temptations of the world and was so proud within, knowing that I had stalwartly and steadfastly upheld the traditions of the community back home.

Then one day, as a proud, young Christian professional nurse with mores intact, I visited back home for ten days at the beginning of the New Year. It was 1966, five years after first having left home. I had never tasted a beer, still went to church twice every Sunday, and had worked hard to make my own way and to be financially independent. Had it been my birthday, I could even have given the class a nickel treat with a little snootiness thrown in for free. I knew achieving the upper echelon status in the community would forever be impossible, but on that visit I remember feeling somewhat more on an equal footing with those folks.

It so happened that my mother worked as the evening manager in the Churchill Retirement Home at which Mrs. Simon Cole resided, and on Sunday afternoon Mom asked me to accompany her on her rounds in the Home. I gladly agreed to do so, and as we walked down the hallways, Mom gave a running commentary on her duties and the people who lived there.

We came to Mrs. Simon Cole's room and Mom said in a hushed tone, "You remember Mrs. Simon Cole, don't you? She is 90 years old. We won't bother her now. Oh, no. She is watching her football and wants nobody to bother her."

I stopped dead in my tracks. Not believing my ears, I repeated the word, "Football?" and immediately followed it with a second incredulous, "*Football?*"

"Oh, yes," answered Mom blithely, "every Sunday; she just loves her football, other ball things, too."

"But on Sunday?"

I pushed forward past my mother to peek into the slight crack of the open door, and sure enough, I could see part of the screen of the T.V. and the football uniforms of the players on the screen. The sights and sounds were inescapable. I knew what it was: the American Football League Championship game, the Kansas City Chiefs against the Buffalo Bills.

Dumbfounded, flabbergasted I spluttered, "Mrs. Simon Cole watches football on television on Sunday?"

"Come, come on, in this room lives Mr. Hoffman. He will have his tea ready. Come, let's go on," Mother urged, obviously not fazed by Mrs. Cole's wickedness. *When had all this changed? Did I even know these people*?

My mother stopped to chat with Marion Drew, another resident, and I was left alone in the stillness of a Sunday in an empty corridor of the Churchill Retirement Home. I saw through a window the spire of the Christian Reformed Church stretching loftily upward into the big sky. I swear, as I reprocessed the startling information that Mrs. Simon Cole watched football on television on Sunday, I heard the sound of mortar cracking and, not long after, the noise of bricks tumbling down. The revelation had punched a hole right through my wall of discipline. In fact, my wall still lies in a shambolic state around my feet, as I write.

Snowbird Stories: Several Degrees Beyond Common Sense

Of course, I'll catch the rest of the football playoffs and the Super Bowl and follow it with the quarter-finals on through the finals of the first of the year, major tennis tournament, the Australian Open, held in Melbourne. After which I will immerse myself in March Madness, the month-long college basketball tournaments. I like both, the men's and the women's. The National Basketball Association playoffs will begin after that; they go on for almost two months. Sometime in June I'll enjoy the tennis matches on the red clay courts at Roland Garros, the French Open, and then Wimbledon on grass in London around the first of July. The women's softball is pretty cool at that time, too. Naturally, I never miss the October baseball playoffs and the World Series, to say nothing of the Olympics every two years. Even golf, the Masters. Now I'm into golf! On a slow day I'll even watch Championship Bowling. So far, thank God, I don't like car racing, hockey, biking—the *Tour de France*—or soccer, although I will catch some World Cup matches if there is nothing else on the tube. Oh, yes, and the athletes in the marathons, the triathlons, I love their amazing endurance.

I'm a skim-the-cream-off-the-top kind of spectator; I go for the best competition: the playoffs, the tournaments, the bowls and such—except for college football; they are on Saturdays and Saturdays, as I've said, are not a problem for me. Carefree, I watch them all day every Saturday as the leaves float down well into autumn, past the cornucopias of Thanksgiving and through the myriad of bowl games at the first of the year.

I am always admiring the fine, fit, sculpted bodies and the incredible courage and concentration. I am rooting for the underdog, anticipating the come-from-behind miracle and hoping for the cliff hanger finish. Like every addict, I am chasing that same exhilarating rush that I felt the very first Sunday I turned on the football game. I'll never forget it: Sunday, September 9, 1967, the new football season, New York Jets 19, the Miami Dolphins 14 and I saw that Joe Namath was as terrific as I had heard he was!

But darn it all, this sullied or tainted feeling that I get in the aftermath of my Sunday high is like an earwig in a yellow rose; it makes the beautiful—and the athletic dance of the young, healthy body *is* a thing of beauty—turn into something ugly, something repulsive even. If I didn't have to deal with this vexing problem, I wouldn't worry at all about being a sports-on-television-on-Sunday junky. I'd be having a great time!

This is my weekly *liet motif*: On Sunday evening—like I am doing tonight—I give considerable consideration to checking myself into rehab and going through some pretty serious detoxification. When I consider it, I instantly start to feel deprived, so then I tell myself that it won't mean quitting cold turkey. *Cold turkey is just not realistic*, I say, *but it could mean something between your all-or-nothing approaches. Remember what they used to teach, what Saint Paul advocated in the Bible: moderation in all things? Now that is a sound Calvinistic principle well worth remembering.* This weekly self-talk helps me to feel a little better, and then the next Sunday it is the same old story. I fall off the wagon. Again. And go through my aftermath litany. Again.

There is a remote possibility, I have thought on occasion as I lie on this Sunday-evening-bed-of-nails, that I am not so much addicted to watching sports on Sunday as I am addicted to the notion that there is a perfect model for what constitutes acceptable behavior on a Sunday—obviously believing at some core level that Sundays should have a measured amount of austerity and misery built in to them. It is even entirely possible, I have gone further to imagine, that Martha Cole did not grow up with my model of perfection, did not view herself as being hooked on something unclean and at 90 years of age was in that Retirement Home room watching all of her "ball things," guilt and shame-free. *If that was the case,* I tell myself ruefully, *I really need to stop blaming the old materfamilias; I just need to take the next step in imitating her. Sports on television on Sunday? Bring it on! God bless America! As I live and breathe, the dearly departed Martha Cole is my role model!*

Chapter Fourteen

People Who Live with Pets Do Better

I AM RESTING IN MY BIG MAN LAZY Boy recliner and Figgy, my soul mate, is pressed firmly and warmly against my right lower leg. Her presence is reassuring—as long as she is with me, I will not feel lonely. I see the tiny gray hairs around her eyes, nose and mouth and notice not for the first time that her whiskers are fewer. It has been a sad day for us.

Dr. Hall, her gnome-like veterinarian here in Mesa, said regretfully this afternoon that she had signs of kidney failure. He loves her, too. He stroked her head and gave her a kiss on top of her head after he said it.

"You can give her three times weekly subcutaneous infusions of Lactated Ringers, a solution of normal saline and electrolytes," he said. "It could possibly extend her life for three to six months. You would just put a needle under her skin on her back and run in 100cc from the I.V. bag. I'll have the technician demonstrate it for you and we'll give her a dose today if you like."

I wished for Sophia's level head, and it didn't occur to me that I could wait to make the life-extending decision until she was back from Detroit.

"Okay," I replied and then brought home the box of supplies.

As I watch Figgy snooze comfortably beside me now, I get flashbacks on our life together.

Snowbird Stories: Several Degrees Beyond Common Sense

It started back in October of 1987, in Maine when I was healing from my mastectomy but before getting sick from the chemotherapy. Someone had given me Bernie Siegel's book, *Love, Medicine and Miracles* where he wrote that cancer patients that have pets do better than those who do not have pets. For me it was a no brainer; I needed to get a pet.

I considered my choices: the teaching job kept me away from home too much to have a dog. I had learned a painful lesson in that regard when I was a graduate student in Boulder, Colorado. A friend had given me a small, black-haired terrier whose paws were white; she had little tufts of white on her ear tips and snout—cute as can be. Niki slept by my shoulder and laid her head on my throat. We breathed in unison, but sadly the high-strung little soul suffered from severe separation anxiety. Daily, I had to come home to torn up clothes on the floor and this poor, crazed creature bouncing off the walls. Time and again my roommate let her get out, and time and again at no small expense to me, I had to retrieve her from the pound. This I simply could no longer afford; I had to give her away and even though another small dog would be sweet, I decided that I was not going to go through that agony again.

Bernie Siegel also wrote that it is the stroking of the pet that is good for the person; therefore, I realized, a bird or fish, though better than nothing, would not suffice. That decided it for me then; a cat was my answer. Without further ado I called Sophia and off we went to the Kennebunk Humane Society. Cancer, you see, can crystallize thoughts and actions in that manner; it's one of its many perks—I also never again have had underarm hair and the hair on my head turned curly: both perks, in my opinion, but that's a bit off point.

Tjaakje C. Heidema

We toured the cat section and I came to a stop in front of one cat in order to see her better. Her tail end was pressed against the very back of the cage and, like a person with post-traumatic stress disorder, she faced determinedly forward to see the whole room and to see any potential threat coming towards her. The card said she was a two-year-old female, short-haired tortoise-shell named Figaro. Figaro? A barber? A bolero or short jacket? Both the opera role and the Disney pet were male, were they not? Maybe that's why she had that deep dark scowl on her face. Maybe somebody named her thinking she was a male and then rejected her when they found out she was female. I'd be ticked off, too.

Despite being drawn to Figaro, I turned away from her cage that day and decided to adopt Paul instead. He was an overtly friendly, gray and white tiger- stripe who waved both furry paws out through the bars of his cage in hopes of attracting some desperately desired human attention and touch. When I held the light-as-a-feather little fellow, he was a love. He snuggled warmly against my chest and put his face up to touch mine. Clearly, he would be a fantastic cancer buster and immune system booster. All the technicians even said it was Paul whom they would adopt if they didn't already have enough cats.

But I couldn't walk away from Figaro's cage; I kept going back and back again. I would bend down and take another good look at her. She had this put upon, annoyed, damn-it-to-hell, steely look—which I have since come to know very well—that drew me, I think. Along with her introverted personality and obvious attitude problem, her fur was dull and matted. Nonplussed by my attraction to this cat, I decided to go with my instinct and announced I would adopt her as well. After all, I had cancer, I reasoned, and it was about time that I listened to my instincts, which, by the way, is another one of the perks. One gets more in touch with one's body and mind and their subtle nudging. Let me say this: if not after a diagnosis of cancer and getting hit upside the head with mortality, then when?

My newly adopted pets came home with parasites so a visit to Dr. Tusch, the Wells veterinarian, was first on our agenda. He loved Paul; said he had "royal bearing". He didn't have much to say about Figaro. Next on the agenda was to begin brushing them. Paul's fur was healthy and a fine texture. Thinking it was a game, he would try to eat the brush. Figaro's fur was thick and she wanted no part of being handled. Every afternoon I picked her up and placed her firmly on a denim cloth on my lap. With my right hand grasping the hide at the nape of her neck, I valiantly tried to brush her with my left. Any lapse of attention on my part and Figaro would dig her claws through the denim into my thighs and catapult off into space. For weeks we were locked into this battle of the wills. I didn't give up; neither did she. She scowled; so did I.

Figgy—a better name than Figaro, I decided—never showed out and out anger in her eyes; it was always just short of such a fiery blaze and filled rather with way more grit and defiance. Indulging in expressions of anger—she either knew innately or had already learned in her first two years of life—was a wasteful exercise. She used the energy, instead, to outlast life's irritants, to survive.

In our other daily activities Figgy and I warily watched each other from a safe distance. When I opened the door for the cats to go outdoors, Paul bounded out with great enthusiasm. He was a people-lover—I would see him in the trunks of the neighbors' cars as they unloaded their groceries—and a natural-born hunter. Figgy, on the other hand, before stepping out would take great pains to sniff the door jamb, the door step and the rubber mat. Not once a day but every single time! Her methodical inspections stretched my patience to the nth degree and I so wanted to give her a polite shove with my foot—cats I grew up with were never coddled; they were barn cats, so for me to let Figgy set the pace was a totally new experience—but I wanted to earn her trust, so I waited and waited.

By January the chemotherapy cocktail of 5FU, methotrexate and citoxin was giving me fits. I was bone-tired, had a nonstop, wicked sinus headache and the worst abdominal cramping. I would sit on the commode, rock back and forth and moan from the bottom of my soul with what I felt was well-deserved self-pity. Paul could have cared less; Figgy watched, I noticed, without her usual air of indifference. I even imagined that she had an expression not of curiosity but of concern on her face.

One such day, to my great surprise, as I was moaning and carrying on, she began to weave around my ankles and rubbed her face and body up against them. The whole time she was urgently peeping— Figgy doesn't meow; she peeps—and there she was, like a little mother hen, fussing mightily over me. How did she know the truth—that I so needed mothering? When I reached down to assure her that I was all right, she rebuffed my strokes and continued her rubbing and peeping. *This is not about me wanting attention,* she seemed to say. *This is about me giving to you.* I was deeply touched; my heart melted and I cried real tears of delight and gratitude. Figgy and I had bonded!

I finished my six months of chemo on Easter weekend and in May was able with the help of Sophia to travel to Pullman, Washington, for the graduation of my niece Sandi from Washington State University

School of Veterinary Medicine. We left "the kids" in the care of our close friends, Lois and Nancy, who enjoyed staying in my house by the sea. Unfortunately, during that time Figgy was attacked by Ivan, the neighborhood bully tomcat, and developed an abscess on her back. Dr. Tusch put in a drain, sewed her up, prescribed antibiotics and I came home to Figgy in a lampshade collar.

When I thought it was safe to remove her lampshade, I discovered that Figgy had been nurturing her own idea about what would make her back feel better. Almost immediately, she twisted her head back around, sank her fangs resolutely and deeply into the wound, shook her head back and forth and tore the offending area wide open! Back to Dr. Tusch; back into the lampshade. Three, four times we repeated this scenario with no end in sight.

Stymied, I remember asking of Dr. Tusch, "Will we end up having to put her to sleep?"

"Oh, no," he avowed. "We'll get through this." *Easy for him to say*, I remember thinking, *but it really comes down to Figgy and me. Somehow, some way if we're going to make it through, we are the ones who are going to have to figure it out.*

The only thing I knew for sure was that Figgy's back at odd intervals would twitch uncontrollably—presumably from nerve irritation or damage. Sometimes, she would ride it out and sometimes, she wouldn't. It was the twitching that caused her to go at it with her teeth with such vehemence; it was then, I deduced, that I needed to intervene. The next time when I took her out of her lampshade, I watched for the first sign of a twitch. When it happened, I raced over to her, vigorously scratched and rubbed her back, and earnestly entreated her with, "Come here, sweetie. It's okay, it's okay. You'll be all right, Figgy." Thank goodness, after a couple of minutes, the twitching subsided and Figgy was fine. We repeated that same scenario over and over and over until one day Figgy, with a severely twitching back, came running to me for a please-fix-it job. That first time I beamed with pride; we were making such progress in the trust department! This became a routine that we ended up doing for years and years hence.

Even the nightly brushings were going well; she no longer catapulted herself off my lap, and though not yet relaxed, she was tolerating the sessions *sans* scowl. The brushings, in addition to a little olive oil drizzled over her Science Diet dinners, had her sporting a beautiful shiny, mat-free fur coat.

During the summer, no longer employed or employable, I was free to make choices about how I spent my days. One of my choices was to take an afternoon walk on weekdays—weekends being far too busy with the coast of Maine tourist traffic—around the neighborhood and along scenic Ocean Avenue. Paul and Figgy would come with me. Paul would race ahead, dive under buildings, startle mourning doves, scale fences and teeter on jagged rocks along the water's edge while Figgy sniffed and sleuthed out trails of other creatures, micro-scoped insects and lagged behind. When I lost sight of either or both, I would call and clap; and, if not too preoccupied with their own agenda, they would come running. The grand finale always came when we returned home. With my hooting and hollering encouragement the cats would chase one another across my next-door neighbor's lawn and up his huge Dutch Elm tree, and so we arrived home.

One day as I was weeding a flower bed, I became conscious of movement in my peripheral field. It turned out to be Figgy; her body was sort of askew. She was tiptoeing sideways and dancing in place all at the same time. Once she had my attention with these antics, she raced—tail up, belly to the ground, legs outstretched—as fast as she could go and ended up in the Elm tree on a far-reaching branch. Of course, like a fool, the whole way I was applauding and praising her vociferously. She stood there proud as a peacock and, I swear, she had this big grin on her face. I was exhilarated; Figgy not only came to me for soothing when her back was acting up but now she was making me laugh. She had a sense of humor!

"You go, girl!"

Laughter really is the best medicine. Apparently, Figgy in her innate wisdom knew this, too. Deeply satisfied by life in that moment, I could feel my errant and poisoned cells smile and heal.

At least ten times a day, Paul would trumpet his arrival from thirty yards away all the way to the front door to be let inside. Everyone in the neighborhood could hear him. Five out of ten times this meant I had to come down from the second story of the house to let him in. A quick bite of food, an even quicker hug and off Cat Warrior would go again. Figgy had her own system. She would lie just under the back of the Toyota in the shade, visible to a certain someone when she looked out the window. Of course, she had me trained—every fifteen minutes or so, I would go to the window to see if she was there. Those two had me coming and going every which way! Self-absorption was out of the question; self-pity impossible.

When I made the decision to go to Arizona the first time, Doug and Betty Ramsdell, who lived a couple houses down and who loved animals, took in the cats. It was a godsend, really. Betty sent lots of pictures: Paul drinking water from the faucets, Paul playing with the feather toy with Doug, Paul snuggling up with Betty under the quilt, Paul sprawling out in the sun room; Figgy sitting on her haunches scowling, Figgy sitting on the deck scowling; Figgy scowling while she was being brushed.

The day I returned to Wells, Paul and Figgy were out on the lawn of the Ramsdell's; Doug and Betty were gardening in their deep bed nearby. I called the cats by name. Paul looked over but made not a move. Figgy raised her head and without hesitation came bounding towards me. In that moment, Figgy showed unbridled joy and happiness at our being reconnected, as did I. It was eminently clear: we had so missed each other! I couldn't imagine leaving her behind ever again.

I knew it was not in Paul's makeup to have to be restricted to a park model trailer or to be on a leash in Arizona. Doug and Betty loved him, they wanted him, and so I relented and said they could keep him. Over the years when we were back in Maine, he would come and visit us—he still loved to snuggle against my chest—and he and Figgy would lie under the car in the shade together. I could hear him trumpet his arrival at the Ramsdell home as he had done at mine. Just as well, Figgy was quite content to be the chosen one in our home.

For sixteen years Sophia, Figgy and I traveled back and forth between Maine and Arizona. Throughout those years, Figgy never skipped a beat. After a fourteen hour trip in the car and on the plane, she would step out of her carrier in our alternate location, do a quick check of the place to insure there were no intruders lurking about, use the litter box, eat and drink and settle in to sleep off her jetlag.

By 2001, my breathing problems had worsened; I had to stop several times to catch my breath going up the staircase in our Maine home. We thought of installing an electric chair track but traveling by air twice a year with oxygen, a cat, luggage and needing wheelchair assistance was becoming a herculean task, too. A huge change needed to be made. Sophia loved her tennis Over 50 League in Mesa, I enjoyed the Sunlife heated pool and Figgy would adapt no matter where she was, so we decided to move towards living full time in Arizona. The first step was to sell "Homestead Harmonies," our beloved home with the ocean view.

On the closing date, everything was spotless. All our furniture with the exception of a T.V. tray in the dining room had been shipped and we were ready to go. At the actual moment, Ms. Figgy sat pensively in plain view under the T.V. tray. Not hiding in a closet upstairs, not outside in the hedge or under the Toyota or the lawn furniture, or on the porch. No, bless her heart, like Ruth to Naomi in the Book of Ruth in the Bible, her message was, "Whither thou goest, I will go and where thou lodgest, I will lodge..."

Since we could not finalize the sale in Wells and fly out of Boston on the same day and because Soph and I desperately needed a few days' rest, we had rented a cabin in Ogunquit. Almost immediately upon arriving, Figgy escaped. We called and called and were stunned to discover a terrifyingly steep ravine behind our cabin. She did not return that night. Devastated—she had never stayed out all night before—I was besieged by recriminations: Had we made a terrible mistake to pull up stakes? It was not worth losing one of our threesome. I should have been content, not reached for more, et cetera, et cetera. For hours I tossed about fitfully; I couldn't sleep. In the morning we received a phone call from Nancy, our friend. Lois had had a heart attack and needed surgery and did we have our television on? Better turn it on. The picture came in just in time for us to see the second plane hit the Twin Towers. It was 9/11. One of the planes had left from Logan

Airport in Boston; and we might have been on that plane!

It was a miserable, rainy day and there was no sign of Figgy. We alternated between watching the national tragedy unfold on television and scouring the neighborhood for a glimpse of her. Our throats became hoarse; we drew up notices and posted them on utility poles. One of the folks told us there were wild animals in the ravine.

A second night went by and again I couldn't sleep. I was seeing bodies falling through the air from the towers and I was steeling myself to face the loss of my dear Figgy. Awash in guilt, I harangued myself with more questions: How could I have allowed such an awful mistake as to let her get out? How could I have disrupted her routine so drastically? How could I doom her to being torn apart by a wild animal? Why does humanity have to have this stupid capacity for self-righteousness and hatred of the other? Is it all just words and subterfuge covering our more basic territorial instinct for survival of the fittest? Is there even a neutral great spirit who is hearing my prayers for the families of those who died, for Lois and Nancy, for the safe return of Figgy?

At daybreak, Sophia's squeal of delight groggily registered in my brain: "I think it's Figgy!" I sat up, looked for a clock—as if the time mattered—and dared to let the light of hope enter my heart.

Sophia unlocked the front door and I heard excited confirmations, "Oh, it is you, darling, where have you been? We were so worried. Oh, Tjaakje, look at who's come home!"

Figgy jumped up on my bed and allowed Sophia and me to hug and stroke her as our tears of relief fell unabated. She was fine, no wounds or limps, no burs or painful stickers in her pads that we could see. Where had she been? It didn't matter; Figgy was back, our unit was intact and we could proceed as planned. Wish that it could have been just so for the families of 9/11. The poignancy of our joy was muted by their loss and uncertainty.

I found that I could not handle the extreme heat of summer in Arizona; so we are still snowbirds. Now, however, in the spring we drive west through the scorching Mohave Desert, up through busy California, north through the rain and snow of the Siskyou Mountains and up into the lush and green of Oregon and Washington. Fifty miles north of Seattle we come to a stop in the Skagit Valley and see again the fertile farmlands of the delta, the islands in the Juan de Fuca Strait and the snowcapped Cascade Mountains. Then in the fall we do it all again in reverse order. Always in tandem, when Sophia and I stop at a rest top to use the facilities, Figgy uses her litter box.

She is content here in Arizona—she sleeps in her condo, a dark corner of our clothes closet, or stretches out in a pool of sunshine on the bed or in the Arizona room. In the evening after the hot days, she likes to lie on the cool cement of the carport; and in the quiet hour before bedtime, she will walk on the street in the park on a leash—but she prefers our Mount Vernon home in Skagit County like she did our home in Wells. Proprietarily, she walks the boundary of our property, stalks insects and lies under the Japanese maple or in the rows of veggies in Sophia's deep beds. She lazily eyes the birds at the feeders but makes no effort to catch one. She is an appreciator of life and holds her predator instincts, like her anger, admirably in check.

It has been eighteen years since my diagnosis of breast cancer and since Figgy and I have been together. It is unbelievably humbling for me to contemplate that somewhere around 800,000 women have died of the deadly disease in those same years! That is only in the United States; in the world 9,000,000 women have died. I claim no special reason for my survival. I know that whatever I have thought, believed, done, eaten or avoided, many of those women thought, believed, did, ate and avoided as well. They wanted to live, too, and I imagine that a goodly number of them also had pets. I have no special formula, no special answers. Another perk of having had cancer is that every day I know that I am incredibly lucky to have survived. Each day of continued life, therefore, becomes a gift; I know there may not be another.

My furry friend, who has been with me so faithfully on this eighteen-year journey and who now sleeps so peacefully against my leg, was two years old when we embarked on this journey together. She is twenty years old now, a grizzled somewhat frail veteran, and like me, she needs infusions to stay alive. We have come such a long way in our relationship. It amazes me after all this time that there is still an occasional layer of defense that we surrender to one another. Just recently, for example, she has let me hold one of her front paws lightly in my hand—a total no-no all these years—and she will occasionally come on her own volition to lie in my lap.

Even more recently, when I supervised her unleashed excursion out back of the trailer and while she did her C.I.A.-worthy sniff job on the neighbor's tool shed, I gratefully felt the sun first thaw and then warm my tight chest while I listened to the complete "Ode to Joy" sung by the purple finch from atop the T.V. antenna. I am still working on letting go of control, fine-tuning the patience thing; but, really, because of Figgy's lessons, I am so much better at it: trusting the process, being in the moment, going with the flow, that sort of thing. They're all perks from having had cancer and from having lived with Figgy.

You and I will go on together as long as we possibly can, I affirmed to her. Relaxed and at peace, I watched her effortless breaths come and go; I saw the tiniest of twitches in her legs as she dreamed of... what? I wondered.

Relationships are never easy for me and there are ways in which over the years I have emotionally hurt friends and family members and they in turn have hurt me, too. But there is no doubt about it! From deep down in my core I know my relationship with Figgy is...well, it's very, very special. I've been good to her and she has been good to me. I love her; she loves me. It's a beautiful thing.

Figgy's life was extended by another two and a half years. She died on March 8, 2008. She was 22 and a ½.

Chapter Fifteen

The Farewell Luncheon Debacle

I REALLY THOUGHT THAT I HAD LEARNED MY LESSON, a lesson that had been taught to me way back in the late sixties when I attended Colorado University and lived in Boulder, Colorado. At the time, incompatibilities with a roommate had necessitated that I move to a different address. Being self-sustaining and very poor, I was fortunate to have found an apartment within my means. It was in an old downtown apartment building—all the interior doors and trim had long ago been stained that dark walnut color and the much worn carpet runner was dark as well. On top of that the hallway was dimly lit, too. Everything was dark and old but, thankfully, neat and clean. There were four other apartments on the same floor.

Almost every day when I came home from school or work, the four older women from those apartments—a couple of whom were always wearing robes no matter what the hour—would be clustered together in the hallway complaining about various and sundry empty boxes abandoned by the unresponsive landlord. To whom did they belong? What might happen in an emergency? Weren't they a fire hazard? Wasn't it against code? Who might be called? Who would care about their concerns? One Saturday, tired of their lymphatic litany of complaints, I made swift work of clearing out the boxes—it wasn't that big a deal; there weren't that many—and I never saw the women talking to one another again.

There I was, taking sociology and psychology classes at the university, supposedly learning about the inner workings of groups and individuals; yet I had, in a few moments of self-serving and blind ignorance totally ruined a social network—possibly a vital one. It saddened me deeply and I thought the lesson learned would be a life lesson: Leave well-enough alone.

But oh no, I am such a slow learner! For the umpteenth time since that lesson I have imposed my will yet again. Today, as I have on every other occasion, I had to suffer the consequences one more time ...yet again. Instead of ruining a social network, however, this time I managed to envision one that did not exist. I organized and tried to pull off a farewell luncheon for Evelyn, a former neighbor.

To me, it seemed like a win-win idea: I would enjoy having lunch out, would feel like an integral part of a group, and would reap satisfaction from having done a good deed. A trifecta, what's wrong with that? The first clue that this might turn out to be a leave-well-enough-alone thing, should have been that Sophia did not agree with me at all. She was not that fond of Evelyn, she said. She had a point; Evelyn can be annoyingly abrasive. Also, Sophia thought that someone who had known Evelyn longer should initiate a luncheon or a cake and ice cream gathering. It took a bit of doing, but eventually I was able to talk her into going along with it. Which reminds me: after I write this, I must thank her for not doing the *I told you so* routine.

Evelyn became a widow last winter and, since I had learned a lot—or so I thought until today—from the widows in my work with the bereavement group through Hospice, I was empathetic. Evelyn didn't ask for anything, mind you; in fact, in retrospect, might not even have wanted anything. She was eating healthily, walking quite a distance every day, involving herself with other people in park activities and generally moving on with her life. It was me; I was trying to help her close this chapter that she had shared with her husband by inviting her to a farewell luncheon. This brings to mind another great piece of advice that I ignored today: it was on a poster I used to have up in my office which said, "If things don't get better soon, I may have to ask you to stop helping me."

Anyway, Evelyn and her husband, Chaun, used to live just down the street here in our park in Mesa in lot #F62. They were part of our neighborly cluster that includes Chuck and Wilma next door in F64 (ours is F66), Tom and Mildred across the street in number 61 and Ed and Jean in 63. Patty in G63 and Marlene in G61—G street is behind us and only four feet or so separate the back ends of our trailers—are also in the cluster. We'd all get together once in a while, usually at Chuck and Wilma's, for some birthday cake, but mostly we chatted with one another in groups of two or three in the street as we came and went.

Evelyn, a strong woman, was handling the loss of Chaun well, we'd been saying up until now. However, last month in some sudden and irreversible decision-making, we said, she had become uncharacteristically passive. And, trust me; we all had a lot to say about that. Just to one another, of course—one doesn't say such things to Evelyn directly; she always acts like she knows exactly what she is doing.

Evelyn is amazingly fit and trim. She has great posture, few wrinkles and a healthy-looking complexion—she insists it is because of the all-natural Shaklee Products that she uses and sells. She dresses confidently in white sneakers and slacks with sporty, comfortable tops. So therefore, it does not seem possible that she will be 82 years old in May. However, despite her well-being and obvious thriving as a snowbird, her son, her only child—as newly promoted head-of-the-family after his father's death apparently—had, at Christmas time, autocratically insisted that she settle into a year-round retirement apartment near him and his family in Colorado. Evelyn, in an unusually compliant—yet complaining all the while—move had impulsively sold her spotless trailer—she still had the original plastic on the easy chairs that she and Chaun had sat on for fifteen winters, for heaven's sake—to a couple of chain smokers with an annoying yippy dog. (Reason enough, Sophia had included in her arguments to me, not to give her a luncheon.) Thus, Evelyn left our F street cluster last month. For the remainder of the season she is renting a trailer on E street and we see her less frequently.

    I started my lunch invitations with Wilma. When I suggested a farewell lunch, she first hesitated, but then —oblivious to my destructive not leaving well enough alone propensity—agreed that it was a good idea. She wanted to be included, she said, as long as we could plan it around her endoscope procedure on Monday and the removal of the bone spur in her foot the following Friday. She would tell and invite Jean from across the street in #F63.

    The following evening and four or five evenings hence Jean, a former schoolteacher and a tiny little bird of a person with fine carrot-colored hair, came to our home to discuss the "nuts and bolts" of the luncheon. She made a new list each time she came over but forgot to look at the list once she had written it down.

    On evening number five, Jean, armed yet again with another new list, asked if she could be the one to invite Mildred. We happily concurred, thinking erroneously that Jean was progressing to a new level. Shortly after she left, we received a phone call from Jean who was with Mildred. Jean wanted to know where, who, when and so forth! Sophia, anticipating Jean's visit the following evening, had a written list ready to go, met her at the door and blocked the opening with her body. A brief discussion was then held outdoors on the landing.

Sophia was shocked at Jean's mental decline. I say I think she was well on her way last year already. Wilma thinks it has something to do with Jean's chest pain and a heart attack sometime in the past. Sophia and I as nurses don't think the two are related but don't openly disagree with Wilma either. Perhaps we're getting old enough to allow that anything is in fact possible.

I scheduled the luncheon on a Saturday so that Marlene could be included; she was "very busy" every other day. "I usually like to keep my Saturday's free from obligations but I can't any other day, so I guess it's all right," she had begrudgingly conceded.

"Not what I would call a whole-hearted endorsement from her either," I had mumbled afterwards to Sophia. "Like we all don't have things that keep us busy." Sophia, to her credit, had said nothing but she did get her message across by emphatically rollind her eyes at me.

When Saturday came, Marlene said she was sick and begged off. Wouldn't you know it? Jean arrived at 11:00, even though her list said 12. Oh, well. Patty was seeing an old classmate, she said, and also would not attend. Frankly, I was relieved: first of all, because Patty is a heavy smoker and second because Patty is mostly responsible for the fact that Evelyn sold her trailer to the obnoxious smokers with the yippy dog.

Snowbird Stories: Several Degrees Beyond Common Sense

Patty hauled over this couple, showed them Evelyn's place while Evelyn was gone and quoted them a price $2,000 less than Evelyn's asking price. Evelyn panicked, thought there would not be any other buyers and—fearing son's disapproval, I guess—fell for it. Now, the smoke-wafting and the dog-yapping irritate the heck out of all of us. Needless to say, we have not welcomed our new neighbors and most likely will not do so for some time to come.

Bev from F 72, who is not in this cluster of ours but who was thoughtfully included by yours truly because she has become Evelyn's buddy since they are both widows—birds of a feather, and so forth—will attend. Mildred will not and only Jean and I care. True, Mildred talks way too much—all the time actually—but I care because I had hoped to feel her hands a second time. The first time we shook hands, her hands reminded me so much of my mother's hands. Mildred, like my mother, I learned, milked cows by hand when she was a young girl. I now recognize that feel and love to shock a woman I am shaking hands with by asking her if she milked cows by hand. Pretty kinky, I realize. I live a boring life; what can I say? I did mention, didn't I, that I wanted to be an integral part of a group?

On this the appointed day, Evelyn arrived at our trailer and announced that she did not like our chosen restaurant—cafeteria style—and would prefer to be served. La-di-da. So, we thought up other possibilities, called a few and settled on a place Bev liked. Sophia and I had never been to Bev's choice of restaurant but, already somewhat beaten down by the process, decided to go with the flow. Evelyn had been there, she said, and it would do. I am peeved. Who exactly gave her veto and approval power? This is a treat from neighbors and friends. not an entourage catering to a prima donna, after all.

When we got to the place, Sunland Village Café, personnel completely overlooked the six of us. We stood around for a while and then assumed that the table one of the waitresses was preparing would be for us. It was not; we had to be more assertive.

Seated at last, at one of the many long tables that held eight, we noted that it was inordinately noisy. It was like a henhouse at sunset; all the folks in the room were chattering at once. Evelyn with two hearing aids couldn't hear a word we spoke. Her brow was furrowed, her mouth set in a straight line and her demeanor apoplectic. We hastened to play musical chairs to find her the best possible hearing spot. All locations, predictably, were noisy but she took a seat that she thought was the best.

Jean, like a sprightly little sparrow, chirped throughout. Evelyn, a bona fide health nut who has taken lecithin for eons and who has a memory like an elephant, became curt with Jean, telling her that she had already heard that certain thing three times.

There were two bouquets of rather tall, dusty, fake flowers on the table. I removed them and placed them on an empty table. Everyone—especially Evelyn—applauded my effort and affirmed that it was much better without them. Inanely, I said to Jean, "Who would have thought that flowers could be that noisy?" Jean thought I was hilarious and the two of us laughed. Evelyn resumed her frowning.

Our waitress was slovenly, unkempt and semi-rude which prompted Sophia to suggest we leave to go to The Sizzler. Ever the compulsive-ruffled-feathers-smoother, I said beguilingly to Sophia, "Let's just try to make the best of it, okay?" Wilma settled it by saying that The Sizzler had closed weeks ago.

We ordered. Bev mentioned to the waitress that Evelyn was having a birthday and asked the waitress to provide the special birthday dessert. The waitress left saying neither yea nor nay about the ice cream, and Jean showed unusual lucidity when she told Bev it was not Evelyn's birthday but Evelyn was leaving. Bev flushed with embarrassment or irritation and said tersely, "I knew that," and half turned her back to Jean. Sophia, Wilma and I hastened to assure Bev that it was easy to make mistakes and Evelyn certainly deserved to have her special dessert anyway. We assured Jean that it was all right to pretend that Evelyn was having a birthday since she would be in Colorado when it really was her birthday. Evelyn, thankfully, had not understood any of the transactions and furthermore wasn't the slightest bit interested.

The slovenly waitress served a dish of vanilla ice cream to Evelyn at the same time that she brought the mediocre-looking, deep-fried chicken strips, patty melts and other sandwiches. Sophia took offense and in a semi-rude manner asked the semi-rude waitress what was she thinking and to please keep the ice cream in the freezer until we had finished with our meal.

Meanwhile, we had more fully assessed our whereabouts and determined that we were at the periphery of a private party of 60 or more people, and they were enjoying a much better-looking buffet than what we had before us! Just as we began to eat, the chairperson of this private party took up a microphone and proceeded to conduct the group's business! We looked askance at one another; Bev, feeling the burden of responsibility, blanched. They were all from Franklin County somewhere up north and the usual, so-much-overused snowbird joke was made about whether or not the last one to leave the county had remembered to turn off the lights. They gave a full weather report on Franklin County's most recent snowstorm, selected a new chairperson and passed the microphone around for introductions. Each man gave his name and that of his "better half", the road they lived on in the county and what their children were doing for work and where they were doing it.

We were outraged but what could we do? Our meal had just begun! Sophia found the manager and complained vociferously—Sophia takes the bull by the horns; me, I lay down and let it trample me—but to no avail. The annual income from the 60 plus Franklin County-ites meeting clearly outweighed our paltry contribution to the manager's coffers. He was undisturbed by our unhappiness. He could not afford, he said, to pay someone to stand outside to tell other patrons that a private party was in progress. Had he never heard of posting a sign?

We gave up on any meaningful conversation and decided to go to Dairy Queen for dessert where we would give Evelyn our small farewell gift. Before departing—oldsters not ever known to pass up a freebie—we secured Evelyn's dish of ice cream from the freezer and passed it around the table. I took a bite too quickly and my forehead throbbed. We went as a group to the cash register and were overlooked again. That is, until Sophia raised her voice.

It was 94° out as we slowly negotiated the busy weekend traffic for four miles to Dairy Queen. We ordered our individual desserts and gathered in a corner booth where loud radio music poured forth from the speaker above our heads. Sophia explained our situation to the manager at the counter and asked if the music could kindly be softened for a short time. The manager would be glad to oblige, she smiled, but was sorry to have to tell Sophia that 50 young soccer players were expected at any minute. Hearing this news, we laughed—all the while keeping an eye on Evelyn's nonverbal expressions so as not to laugh too raucously—at the comedy of errors and tried to keep on a good face. Sure enough, in the next minute young soccer players and parents were swarming all over the place.

Midst the mayhem, Evelyn opened her gift, a six-inch glass cactus, thanked us once—*sans* ooos and ahhhs—and brusquely put it aside. A short while later—with heads huddled in towards the center so that we could hear—we attempted to have a go-around on how each of us first met Evelyn. Jean couldn't remember the city or the year but was sure she had known Evelyn for a very long time. When that was finished, Evelyn launched into telling us about a Dateline program on television. Bone meal from cows, she reported, showed traces of the disease that cannibals had; it was causing people to have holes in their brains. We all concurred that was awful, just terrible, scary, and a sign of the times. I took the initiative to say that we certainly couldn't end on such a dire note and told a joke about a priest and a minister. Born-again Evelyn wasn't at all sure she liked the joke but Jean still thought I was hilarious. The future soccer stars of America were rehashing and hollering play by play accounts to one another across the room.

Numbed into a strained silence at last, we leaned back against the bench. Not one of us said a word when Evelyn announced that she would most likely come back to Sun Life next year. She would rent a place, she said. Poor Jean became hopelessly confused by Evelyn's announcement and I just didn't have it in me anymore to make her laugh.

On the way home, when Evelyn and Sophia were shopping in the grocery store—Sophia to buy a half gallon of Cream 'n Cookie ice cream per request of Marlene who didn't feel like eating anything else today, and Evelyn to buy, Lord knows why, Q-Tips—and with Jean's little spirit having given way to sadness, the rest of us sat quietly in the stifling heat in the van.

After an extended pause, Wilma said that as long as she had known Evelyn there was one thing she had never liked about her: "It's that she always has something negative she has to talk about, and it can really get to be too much."

I reflexively started to silver-line it by saying that I thought it was because she was grieving, but in midstream, realized that Wilma's assessment was dead on: Evelyn's curmudgeon stance with Jean, with us, and with life in general had nothing whatsoever to do with grief. It was a persona, an unpleasant persona, which I had foolishly determined to overlook. *What is it about reality that makes me want to change it into something different?* I began to ruminate.

Three hours from the start of what could only be called a grand debacle, Sophia and I fell exhausted onto our beds. She was snoring in a minute or two. Me? I reran the tape in my head and then asked myself yet again, *Why do I engage in this kind of nonsense? Is it the winds of bad karma swirling around me from a prior existence? Is it the vibrations from these red, rocky outcroppings here in the desert? More likely, it was just an altruistic act tossed about in the great sea of random events. No, not true,* my ever-present self-effacing internal voice remonstrated, *you should have known better; you should have left well enough alone!*

Chapter Sixteen

End of Life Issues

LYING COMFORTABLY ON MY BACK on the stretcher, I lazily let my head loll to the left and looked out through the small window. There were golden streams of sunlight reflecting off the brilliantly-bright silver wing of the airplane; below were huge puffy white clouds and above, a limitless blue sky. Transfixed, I watched a majestic mountain slip slowly into view. *If the window were open,* I remember thinking, *I could extend my arm and sweep my hand right across the peak of Mount Rainier; it seems that close.* With each inspiration then, I dared to breathe a little deeper, and with each exhalation, I found I could release a bit of my pent up emotions. I blinked and a tear fell on the pillow.

The way I imagine a just released inmate—who had been incarcerated for a crime she didn't commit—must feel is how I felt: grateful, humbled, cautiously ecstatic, inexplicably ashamed, diminished, afraid, and already feeling the freedom heal my broken spirit. That last one was the amazing miracle. On the calendar it happened to be Good Friday but, as far as I was concerned, it was my resurrection day, my Easter.

"Will you need to nebulize before we land?" asked the flight nurse.

We—me, the flight nurse, Sophia, Figgy in her carrier, the pilot and copilot—were purring along at 625 mph in a private Lear Jet owned by Advanced Air

Ambulance. The pilot said we had been as high as 46,000 feet but soon after crossing the Oregon/Washington border had started our descent. Seemingly only minutes after seeing Mount Rainier, I watched Puget Sound and the Space Needle slip by as well. We would soon be landing at Payne Field in Everett, Washington.

"This is how we will do it," said the nurse. We'll lift your stretcher out of the plane and lower you down onto the tarmac near your brother-in-law's van. From there we'll help you to stand and then help you into the seat."

"Sounds good," I replied. "With your help getting up I can stand and then with support I can walk."

All went as planned and soon after the drive from Everett to Mount Vernon we pulled into Little Mountain Estates double-wide mobile home park off Section Street. The popular plum trees along the circular drive were in full bloom, pink and white blossoms serenading dark trunks and branches absolutely gorgeous. Daffodils had gone by but the Tulip Festival was just beginning.

It was 2007 and Sophia's, Figgy's and my snowbird days were officially over. It wasn't like we hadn't planned for the change; we had. Much like batteries losing their juice after a lot of use, we had finally become exhausted by our two-home, two-culture lifestyle—all the closing and openings, the packing and unpacking, too much. We had, in fact already sold our Mallard park model, "the Duck" as we liked to call it, in Sun Life in anticipation of this day and had been renting it back from the new owners for our final months in Arizona. What we had not planned for was it ending in quite this fashion. To have traveled in a private Lear Jet to the tune of $16,000 for two and a half hours of flight was not exactly do-able at our pay scale, but it was the only way to get me sprung from the joint, so to speak.

It all started in January. Every January that I lived in Mesa I would have an exacerbation of my respiratory problems and this year was par for the course. I blamed the annual witch's brew of trapped pollution from after-the-holidays-lets-go-golfing snowbird traffic and an atmospheric inversion, the dust in the air from winter farming and from excavating dirt to lay foundations for the out-of-control developments, the fireplace burnings—yes, it does get cold on the desert at night—and pollen. It was a diabolic recipe for coughing, wheezing and increased shortness of breath. I had a bad case of all three throughout February and this time around the usual antibiotics and once a week solu-medrol (intravenous steroid) treatments, were not cutting it.

On Friday March 9th, like every other week, I went to the Ambulatory Treatment Unit at Banner Baywood Hospital for my infusion, but for once, Christine, the fun-loving staff nurse, and Linda, the head nurse who is even more fun-loving—she speaks with any one of five fake foreign accents—were not kidding around. They agreed; I did not sound good.

"You should go to the Emergency Department and get a chest x-ray," they insisted.

I didn't want to: John and Elinor Bethke from Alamosa, Colorado were coming to visit and we had made plans to have dinner at P.F. Changs. So instead of listening to them, I went home after my infusion. Yet, I knew I was in trouble; it was two p.m.; okay, I would relent; Sophia and I would go. Maybe an x-ray would reveal pneumonia or something treatable.

I have no idea what would have happened if I had toughed it out and not gone to the E.R.: there might not have been a story to tell or I might not have been around to tell what story there was. Anyway, what did happen was a month-long, mind-boggling melodrama that wreaked havoc on my denial, my psyche and my right leg. All from which I am still recovering. At the outset let me give a word to the wise: if you need the Emergency Room for breathing problems call 911; do not walk in on your own steam!

First, upon walking into the E.R., Sophia and I encountered what we assumed was a triage person standing self-importantly at his little podium. He did not look at me but punched data—which I supplied—into his laptop computer atop the podium. He instructed me to submit my insurance cards to the person behind the glassed-in window who in turn instructed us to enter the door at our left and to sit and wait. We did as told.

For a couple of months we had been hearing that hospitals all throughout the greater metro area were filled to overflowing and it was the case on that day; we sat at least ten deep in rows in the waiting room and some people had to stand for lack of seating. In our midst a slumped over person in a wheelchair was completely covered with a bath blanket; she or he, for all we knew, could have been dead. A diabetic man had an irregular heartbeat, he said, and needed his insulin; he had been waiting for four hours and was afraid of losing his spot if he went home to get it. A young kid with a younger wife had a dirty and bloodied towel wrapped around his hand; he was pale—from the pain, I assumed—and clutched the swaddled hand to his chest. The man next to me was sound asleep, leaning far over to one side and his intravenous bag was empty, dry as a cork. Speaking of being dry, there was no water or anything else to drink. Sophia, the Queen of two planets, Veggies and Fluids, was having a fit about it.

People all around me were snuffling, sniffling, sneezing, coughing and hacking; I kept tissues in front of my nose and mouth so as not to breathe in more bugs than I already had and joined the hacking club. In fact, I could barely speak without setting off paroxysms of dry, rasping noises. Every ten minutes Sophia threatened to make a scene and between wheezes I begged her not to. I heard a litter of kittens mewing in my chest and the more I wheezed, heard and saw the more I coughed and the more I coughed the more anxious I became. Never before had there been a more urgent need for my emergency anti-anxiety pill, Xanax; I popped a couple.

Finally a medical person, a nurse came to assess me and, lo and behold, she didn't look at me either! She read what the first guy had put on the computer from her own laptop.

"What medications are you on?" she wanted to know. I handed her my list and she was pleased as punch that she could just go copy it and put it right into the computer. Off she went never to be seen again.

We had waited three hours before Sophia resolutely reached her limit. She marched up to the desk and insisted on speaking to a doctor. The in-charge M.D. half listened to her and looked me up in his desktop computer. He conferred with a nurse.

"It won't be long before we'll have a cubicle open up," he announced.

"It better be," I heard Sophia retort brusquely, "her breathing is getting worse and worse and if anything happens I am blaming you."

Another hour went by before I was ushered to the back, breathing problem having trumped racing heart diabetic, macerated hand, dry I.V. and possibly dead person. My heart broke at the cruelty; very few people have a Sophia.

Back in the cubicle the staff person took my pulse and announced that I was "tachy". My blood pressure, too, was high, she declared. *Four hours, and these findings are a surprise to you? Better not take Sophia's until she calms down*, I muttered silently as she listened to my noisy breaths with her stethoscope. Multiple tubes of blood were then drawn by a respiratory therapist who seemed an odd person to be doing so. Why not a phlebotomist?

"Not enough phlebotomists available," she explained, "and we can't wait that long."

Now we're in a hurry? Or not. Another hour of waiting went by before the in-charge M.D., without once having applied his stethoscope to my chest, came in to give us his verdict, "Your carbon dioxide level is dangerously high and you could go into respiratory arrest at any minute." Also, he casually commented, "If this exacerbation doesn't get you then the next one will; it is that bad."

I was stunned. *If I am that seriously ill, Doctor of Doom, where were you five hours ago!*

"No chest x-ray?" I asked numbly.

"What for?" he answered. "I have to admit you to the hospital," he continued reluctantly, "but you'll have to wait for an empty bed."

Another hour crept by. The respiratory therapist came with a nebulizer for me to use but otherwise we were left alone in our cubicle. Sophia was starved but didn't dare to leave me now. She was getting in touch with her inner pit bull and talking about a lawsuit; I tried unsuccessfully to soothe her. Eventually we were shuttled into an empty adjoining wing of some sort from which one staff member unpredictably came and went. My possible respiratory arrest, we were led to assume, was not really something in which staff wanted to participate. John and Elinor magically appeared—I never did ask how they found us—and John went to get us a bite of food while Elinor and I compared notes on the latest news about our graduate school classmates. How else to spend the last hours of one's life, if that is what they were to be? Finally, someone came to wheel me to the sixth floor. It was ten p.m. when I finally began a rigorous regime to clear my chest and get the CO_2 level down in my blood.

At frequent intervals around the clock I breathed into a Bi-pap ventilating machine, wore a percussion vest and nebulized with mucomyst and albuterol. I was shot up with whopping doses of solu-medrol and as a result was flying higher than a kite on a windy day. I soaked up the attention and talked nonstop to hordes of foreign staff members: India, the Philippines, Guatemala, Pakistan, Belize are those I remember; traveling nurses in the desert for three months of warm weather were from all the northern tier of cold weather states. Each had their specialty; each had their story. Like the heir apparent to Barbara Walters, I worked at them to expose their secrets. They loved the attention, too, but before long I became disgusted with my insatiable prodding. I knew I should focus on my own needs but soaring too high to stop myself. It wasn't just my anxiety and the solu-medrol high, it was also my elevated Co_2 blood level. It was signaling distress to my brain; my brain in response was kicking into panic mode and pumping in more adrenaline. Hey you, you want to fight or flee? I asked for more and more Xanax and they happily gave it to me. We were having a good time.

On Saturday morning Hospitalist M.D. # 1 came in, stood eight feet away from the bed and asked me if I knew how bad my lungs were? I didn't respond; I just stared at him. He went on: they are very, very bad, he said.

Well, I'll be darned, doc, and here I thought there was still an Iron man Triathlon in my future, I thought sarcastically. *Of course, I know how bad my lungs are! After all, aren't I the one who's been slowed down to a sloth-like pace and the one whose cheeks puff out with pursed-lip breathing to keep my bronchial tree from collapsing? Neither of which, I might add, is much of a fashion statement, but then again, doc, they may be on the planet you've come from.*

"You are in end stage emphysema," he continued "and you should think about end of life issues."

Well thank you for your contribution, Doctor Gloom; you who have known me for all of two seconds! You, Hippocratic wise one, should have that cold heart of yours heated up in a microwave. Clearly, I reasoned internally, *my old reptilian brain is kicking into a higher gear; the meds must be to blame for these thoughts.*

"What was wrong with that guy? Who reared such a sadist?" I asked Elinor who had come up to say good-bye and who shook her head in mutual disgust.

"Don't pay any attention to him," she advised.

I was percussed, nebulized and shot up Saturday and Sunday with no noticeable change. Monday morning a Social Worker wearing a long, starched white lab coat wanted to know if I were to be discharged would I be able to go home or should he start looking for a rehabilitation bed? He was tall, good-looking, intently serious, and a relatively young guy. *I must be gentle,* I thought. He had been charged by the administration, he said, with opening up hospital beds; there was a terrible shortage. I told him as politely as I could that I was not going to be going anywhere just yet; I had end of life issues to think about. "Think about my question anyway," he exhorted.

Tuesday, day number four, aforementioned Social Worker repeated visit and question. No, I had not thought about it; my mind was mush. I never slept; I was on lots of meds. Later I whined to my pulmonologist, Dr. Amy, about the pressure for discharge and she said she would "nip it in the bud." She wanted me to stay in the hospital for the week at least, maybe longer, she said. "I think you need to be here." Then she reported with a smile that she was excited about going on vacation for ten days.

Day number five, Social Worker was at my door again. Apparently there had been no nipping in the bud as promised. I told the now dour, looking older and more haggard fellow, who obviously was shielding himself with that lab coat, the news from Dr. Amy and he said he would check with Dr. Amy's replacement if there was one. Meanwhile he would research bed availability in other facilities. I wanted to tell him rather to research why he wore the lab coat but instead asked him to look into getting a Bi-pap machine at home for me because that was where I was going, home. Clearly, this relationship was heading south; major communication problems were already squelching my earlier physical attraction.

Thursday, day six, desperate for some peace and quiet, I listened to a relaxation tape, but, wouldn't you know it, just as I started to settle down mentally, my bladder delivered an urgent message. I threw off the headphones, leapt out of bed—as much as I was still able to leap, imagine here a sloth leaping—huffed and puffed to the bathroom door, through the doorway and promptly crashed to the floor. Unable to catch my breath, I waited and hoped it would return to me. Eventually it did and I tried to get up but couldn't. With several more tries and a lot of dismay, I learned that it was hopeless; I had to pull the emergency cord. Ever conscious of our image-is-everything culture I covered myself best I could with the too short, too flimsy gown and discovered I was sitting in a puddle: I had peed on the floor. I must have blacked out, I surmised. Oh, God, could anything be more embarrassing? Actually, yes, but I will spare you those too personal details. I pulled the cord and waited. Five, ten, fifteen minutes went by before someone realized there was an emergency light blinking. Two people squeezed into the little bathroom with me and unceremoniously hauled me up by the armpits. Could I walk? Oh, sure, I responded, thinking I probably sounded like whatever a druggie on crystal meth would sound like. Yeah, I was fine, I insisted.

I was not fine. By evening my thigh hurt and was becoming increasingly more painful. They had taken an in-bed x-ray to make sure I had not broken a hip or my femur, so that had been ruled out. The next morning Sophia looked at it—no one else was interested—and saw the beginning of a very large bruise. There was more bruising on my back and hip.

"Tomorrow I am bringing in a camera," she declared. "It will be a lawsuit and I'm not kidding! Do you know that now you have a golden leaf pasted on your door?" she said with disgust. "It means you might become a falling leaf; it tells the staff that you are at risk for falling. Can you believe it? It's too late; where are their heads? With all those meds on board you should have had help all along when getting up!"

Hospitalist M.D. # 2 thought I was bleeding into my quads and would order a circulatory study. "I'm curious," stated Sophia doing her own impression of Ms. Walters. "Why are you a Hospitalist rather than work in private practice?" "Because I am single and like to party," he replied. "This weekend I am going to Madrid; it is a fantastic place to party." Okay, that was a refreshing change from Drs. Doom and Gloom.

By Friday evening I was prostrate with pain. On call Hospitalist M.D. #3 wanted me to have an M.R.I.—the results of the circulatory study had either been irrelevant or forgotten, its initiator most likely pleasantly buzzed and already having group sex in Spain. I told the nurse that I could not manage getting into a wheelchair, up on and off a table, back into the wheelchair and back in bed. She would get an order for pain. At midnight I was pleasantly zonked on a shot of Morphine, lying flat on my back on a gurney and studying the construction of the ceiling in a darkened corridor outside of the imaging room in the bowels of the hospital. "It will take me a while to read and graph this," the tech had said.

"That's all right," I remember responding dreamily. "It is nice and quiet down here."

Besides surveying the ceiling tiles, I lay there a long time marveling at how I could be hyped and zonked at the same time and that Morphine was a powerful respiratory depressant. More importantly, I marveled at the fact that I didn't seem to care one wit if my respirations were depressed to where they might cease all together. Morphine, I was learning, was a heck of a lot better than Xanax or maybe it was the combination of the two that was so lovely.

On the second Monday morning, having survived with morphine on board the whole weekend, I first told even-more- serious-and-not-at-all-good-looking-any-more Social Worker to get off my back and then I asked for some Depends. I was taking the bull by the horns—#2 in Madrid could just come back; didn't need to pay to catch a bull fight over there when he could see one for free in my room; just throw me the red cape.

I told a nurse, "My leg is not functioning; I can no longer lift it, I don't want to get on a bedpan for fear that it will cause more bleeding and the commode is much, much too low. I cannot get up from it! I am putting myself on bed rest."

Capitalizing on my sudden burst of assertiveness, I also warned, "And if we don't start regulating my cocktail of meds—every hour or two I was being given one or more of the following: Percocet (for pain), sublingual (under the tongue) morphine, also for pain, Xanax, Solu-medrol, two different antidepressants, one for sleep and the other to wake me up, and Ibuprofen for inflammation—they are going to kill me." Knowing that my warning was for naught, I maniacally made a large chart for what meds I should have and when. Somebody had to do it.

"This is a great idea," enthused yet another nurse as she taped my inspired chart on the wall.

Still on a roll the next day, I asked for my Case Manager to discuss some aspects of my nursing care but, most importantly, I wanted her help in getting the Bi-pap machine at home at the trailer so I could avoid being sent somewhere else. What I had learned was that I had to be discharged from the hospital first. Then schedule and spend a night in the hospital's sleep center so that they could test me, and if I qualified then I could get a machine at home. I insisted to Ms. Case Manager that certainly there was all sorts of documentation in my chart by now that showed I was more than qualified.

Time and again she emphasized, "There is nothing I can do; that is the procedure," and finally followed that with what I recognized as a frequently used brush-off maneuver: "I will read your chart and come back." *Yeah, right,* I thought. *It's the old tried and true Peter Principle; you have clearly been promoted to your level of incompetence.*

That evening and the next day, Wednesday, my new attitude—filled with that heated mixture of anger and assertiveness, as it was—fizzled and died. Instead of feeling stronger with each day, I was feeling weaker; instead of settling down, I was becoming more shaky, light-headed and breathless. I was using less medication so I could not put the blame there. Where then? I was flummoxed; what was happening to me?

Nonetheless, late that same evening Hospitalist M.D. #4 detached my Bi-pap ventilating machine from the wall outlet. "You don't need it anymore," he announced not listening to a word I was saying about how I was feeling. Thursday morning, I nonverbally told the now downright ugly and evil Social Worker to go take a flying leap—in a civilized manner, of course—after which he handed me a list of nursing homes. Three on the list were highlighted in bright pink.

"They," he explained "accommodate respiratory people."

After he left, I pulled out the hospital's Patients' Bill of Rights and located the phone number for the Patient Advocate. I set up a meeting with her. Friday morning of week two, Sophia, Patient Advocate and I faced three nurses—day nurse, charge nurse and unit supervisor—and the stinking-albatross-around-my-neck Social Worker. I began low-key with a complaint or two; Sophia insisted that when she was a nurse, she did things differently and then I brought up the Bi-pap machine issue and about going home.

"Yes, you must be discharged," they agreed in response, "but we don't think you are able to go home. Medicare will no longer pay for your care here"—what care? I wanted to scoff, but didn't; Sophia did it for me—"and if you stay you will have to pay for it yourself." Social Worker announced self-importantly that he had selected the Springdale West Rehabilitation Center and they would take me at 5 p.m. Sophia stuttered; I spluttered. We were in shock; they were a united front. Our patient advocate took notes.

"Someone from the rehabilitation center"—a euphemism for nursing home, I just knew it—"will be getting you," they said.

"You're going to send her on a Friday night with the weekend coming up?" yelped Sophia—she reminded me of the loyal and fiercely protective miniature Doberman pincher down on F Street in Sunlife who regularly intimidated all of us with his vehement protestations and lunges—"you must be kidding me! That is the worst possible time! Can't you people get anything right?" The united front didn't budge, but eventually I caved.

Eschewing the discharge-against-medical-advice option, I made the tough decision. "I don't want to be here anymore," I told Sophia firmly, "and feeling the way I am right now, my leg the way it is and no Bi-Pap, I don't think I should be going home either. I'll go to this other place."

At five in the afternoon, I lay in bed with my few belongings stuffed in plastic bags next to me. At five forty-five a man in a red jumpsuit, "from the home" he said, came with a wheelchair.

"No!" exclaimed Sophia. "She is **not** going in a wheelchair! She needs a stretcher. Didn't they tell you?"

He didn't have a stretcher; he would have to get a transportation service. He left and we waited. And waited. There was no dinner tray. At eight p.m. a nurse from India, came in and reported that I would not be going. Instead, I would be receiving two units of whole blood throughout the night.

"**What**? You can't have the right patient!"

Hospitalist M.D. #5, she said, had reviewed my blood work before writing the discharge order and discovered that my hemoglobin was very, very low.

Much too low. According to him the bleeding out into my thigh and hip had depleted the blood volume in the rest of my body. No wonder I was light-headed shaky and weak!

I had another sleepless night with checks and changes in the blood drips and bags, percussion with the vest, breathing with the nebulizer and so forth. My head was spinning. *Certainly, the rehabilitation place will not be as traumatic as this place has been,* I naively assured myself.

The next day, Saturday, I was transported to Springdale West. My aide from Jamaica was a self-proclaimed pot-smoking comedian. His idea of work was to make people laugh and not much more. Not that he wasn't a nice change of pace, he was, but all of sudden I desperately missed my strenuous medical regimen. Everything, they said, was on hold until their doctor wrote the orders. Somehow, I made it through the night *sans* regimen.

The morning pills, vital signs and hallway noise began at four a.m. At six thirty there was a loud voice and a lot of racket at my door. In came a hugely obese woman violently pushing a Hoya Lift in front of her. With each of her slams and bangs, the heavy chains of the lift clanked loudly against the sturdy steel bars of its frame and against the door jamb; inevitably, I figured, she was leaving dents and gouges in her wake. She complained bitterly to a cohort about her unfair schedule as she—without so much as a word of explanation—lowered the bedside rails, lowered the bed to where it was flat and with one mighty rough thrust rolled me over to the side away from her.

"I can stand on a scale, if you'll...," I protested knowing as a nurse the purpose of this procedure. "This is easier, honey," she interrupted and snorted with a demeaning tone.

The canvas had large hooks attached to each end and she pushed one end of it firmly under my back and hip and then brutishly rolled me onto my other side facing her. She pulled the canvas through and in doing so unkindly pressed me into her voluminous abdomen. From where I flew into bronchospasm after bronchospasm from the fumes of her cheap perfume. As I gasped and coughed, she shoved me onto my back. She then maneuvered the large triangle-shaped frame over top of me jarring the bed as she hit wheels of lift against wheels of bed and hooked the two ends of the canvas to the chains. Still grousing and grumbling all the while to her compatriot—who was standing by just to lend an ear, apparently—the woman cranked the lift just like she was jacking up a car. I felt myself ascend. I tried desperately to keep my body straight but failed miserably; I didn't have the strength. My legs flailed and fell on one end; my head, shoulders and upper back faltered and flopped on the other. I was in a very unnatural bend and literally could not inhale; I feared I had breathed my last breath and coughed my last cough. Never in my wildest dreams had I imagined it would end like that. Tears flooded my eyes as I imagined being denied my yearned-for-death with dignity.

In the blur of days that followed there was unending noise from blaring televisions at all hours, people talking, laughing and hurrying by in the corridor, rattling carts, cold, smelly food which all smelled the same and vaguely like a petroleum product, the plethora of medication errors, the late breathing treatments, the unanswered lights, the myriad of workers, the hot, stuffy air and the window that looked out on asphalt and that couldn't be opened because of exhaust fumes from vans, cars and buses coming and going underneath the overhang. Sleep deprived for so long, I was unable to concentrate on anything anymore. Even sports on television were of no interest to me. I had been flying high as a kite, but as the steroid medications were steadily being decreased, my kite was hovering just above ground and was about to crash in a sunken heap.

"Will I ever enjoy nature again?" I wailed to Sophia. "I don't think I'll ever leave here!"

"Yes, you will," she said adamantly. "You can't give up hope; keep telling yourself this is only temporary. I'll get you out of here some way, trust me."

It took us ten days but, by God, she—or rather we—did get me out of there. My niece Arlyce and younger sister, Margaret, helped pack, clean and close up the trailer for the new owners and Margaret drove our van up to Washington. Despite a panic attack and dangerously high blood pressure, Sophia, with the help of the Patient Advocate and "in lieu of a lawsuit," she said, even convinced the hospital Risk Management Team to reimburse us for the Lear Jet ride to Everett! What a woman...

Dr. William Osler, known as the Father of Modern Medicine, once said—or is said to have said—"Ask not what disease the person has, but rather what person (and significant support person, my words) the disease has." As I fine-tune this story in 2011, four whole years after my hospital and Springdale West stay in 2007, I can really relate to Dr. Osler's point of view. The Doctors Doom and Gloom didn't know me and they sure as heck didn't know Sophia!

My leg will forevermore be stiff and numb, will have what feels like hot needles poking into it, and will be unreliable. But I can walk unassisted and that's what matters. I have not again needed a Bi-Pap machine or a hospital. My wills, living and otherwise, are complete and current. My power of attorney and beneficiaries are designated and my cremation is prepaid. Now the only end-of-life issues I concern myself with are: What delicacy—Sophia and I call it a "crumpet" for fun—shall we have with tea? Do we have enough dark chocolate on hand? When will be a good time this week for us to recharge our batteries by plugging into nature? And what new road have we not yet traveled?

Ah, life is good.

Some Poetry

Tjaakje C. Heidema

A Glance at Intimacy

After a gentle, warm rain,
crawling in the wet garden dirt
on my knees
and in shirtsleeves,
I come upon two night crawlers
locked in a passionate overlap.

I turn my flashlight hastily away,
blushing to find such
earthy, naked lovers
in their brown bed.

Learning an Ancient Lesson

Not familiar with the lessons of history
and without paths of ancient people
to follow
through deep
mountains and thick trees,
I walked for miles in clouds and fog.

How can I be one
with the rhythms that I hear,
one with the gurgling stream
as it cuts
through the rocks,
one with the sun as it shines
through the cool, blue-green pines?

At the end of the day
too tired to still be afraid,
peace fills my emptiness
and I become one with the quiet pool.

Tjaakje C. Heidema

Between Myself and the Ocean

Between myself and the ocean I've longed for,
are corrals crowded with long-haired,
mud-caked animals—
buffalo, musk oxen, wart hogs
elephants and stallions—
pacing and milling on mounds of frozen manure.

The ice is stained yellow.

They are hungry, grunting
and bare their teeth.
The shrill screams are warnings.

Crouched down, looking through rough boards
and matted haunches,
I catch glimpses of the sparkling waves
and healing sun.
I begin to feel the warmth of the sand against me.

To have these, I must walk through, quickly.

When I awaken from the dream and realize
it won't be as easy as that,
a hot rage grows in my chest and my nostrils flare.

Snowbird Stories: Several Degrees Beyond Common Sense

Die Quietly
(An opposing view with a nod to Dylan Thomas)

An old, tired tree
in the yard
is shedding its leaves
on my lawn
much too soon—it is barely June.

Each leaf has brown spots
splattered on green
like the brown stain on my white-painted wall
when the lid of the stain was tapped
back in place too eagerly
—and, of course, is there permanently.

The tree makes me reflect
on the ninety-two-year-old woman
who sits in her chair
alone in her home
while the lump in her breast grows.
This woman told her nurse, so she knows,
and the nurse told no one but me.

For the young and the hard
this woman and that tree
would be challenges
to cut right into, quite literally.
The two of us, however,
the nurse and myself,
we will wait
and let them die
as they wish—ever so quietly.

Tjaakje C. Heidema

The Thin Line

Bending from the waist
with blood rushing to my head,
then crawling on hands and knees,
while pressed against a shed,
I worked steadily to set free
from grass and weed, a budding Iris
I yearned to see.

Later in the day,
with debris piled high in pails
and dirt still imbedded
in my nails,
you came with your noisy
weed-eating machine
and thoughtlessly shred my Iris dream.

No joy left then with which to fill;
my hands stupidly searched for something
I, too, might kill.
Clenching, but not making a sound,
I wrestled the rootstalk from the ground.
Nothing was left then in that place but pain,
And I stood right there and screamed it all out without
shame.

Snowbird Stories: Several Degrees Beyond Common Sense

Wild Strawberries

Buried in the tall, untamed grass
are clusters of tiny wild strawberries.

It is easy to look quickly,
with a wide sweep of the hand
and to say, "There are none here."

I understand:
it is harder to bend
one's back and legs,
part each swatch of grass
slowly
and look deeply
into those cool, dark places,

waiting for the eyes to adjust.

But if you do then suddenly
you will see
small splashes of red
hanging just above the black
moist soil

in the same place where you saw
nothing
just a moment before!

Tjaakje C. Heidema

The Cosmic Mood

God chose to cast the world
in shades of gray today.
I guess it's okay
because I also feel that way.

You see,
the colors are made
with the warmth and light
of the sun,
and, when God
is in the mood for fun,
all the landscape is painted
before day is done.

But when God
is in a reflective frame of mind,
don't you find,
our world becomes similar in kind?

Snowbird Stories: Several Degrees Beyond Common Sense

Two Miracles

Seeing a splash of orange
fluttering
in a bush,
sends her squealing
for binoculars.

All civilized forms of speech
gone,
she grabs my arm
and stutters excitedly,
"It's a __, over__, look__!"

Joyful, natural woman
bright, beautiful Baltimore Oriole,
two miracles at once
in a split second of time,
both images forever mine.

Tjaakje C. Heidema

Storm of Love

How gently doth the wave
caress the stone,
tear-filled eyes
looking deep into quiet home,
hands touching
naked curves,
desire pressing foam to bone.

So I felt you come
to me
as the storm
of love
passed
and calm prevailed
again
—at last!

Snowbird Stories: Several Degrees Beyond Common Sense

In Praise of the Forest Monarch
(Cedar Walk, Glacier Park, Montana)

People have beaten
a path
around the Forest Monarch,
compacting her roots,
stripping her bark.

Yet, she grows
and rules
reaching for the sun
high above the shadows.

This sovereign cedar will die
one day
from age
lightening or a beetle,
or from one more fatal footfall.

But she wastes no time
fending off death;
she lives
and grows instead.

I, too, then will stand tall,
so with the Forest Monarch
I may feel
the healing surge of the sun
high above the shadows.

Tjaakje C. Heidema

Lois: Goddess of the Coldest Winter Morning

I wake,
open the drape
and see black skeletons of trees
in the steel, still dawn of a freeze.

The wind sighs and groans
along with the cough and the hurt
that's in my chest and in my bones.

Alone in my bed,
I sit up, look out and wait
because I know
that you are coming—
at least that is what you said.

I shiver.

Then, just then,
your car bounces around the leafless hedge,
its hardened suspension creaking
over frozen ruts,
tires shattering
ice on old grey puddles.

"It will be very early
before work.
I will just put the soup by the door,"
you said.

Snowbird Stories: Several Degrees Beyond Common Sense

Goddess... (Cont'd)

I want to hurry
but, "Damn!" I cannot hurry
down the staircase
to that heavy cape
those sheepskin boots
that earthy hug.

I get there eventually but
the cape, boots and hug are all gone;
you have already gone.

Only bits of dirty Styrofoam swirl
in the dry dust
driven by a fierce Artic blast.

I close the door;
your pan of soup is warm
in my hands
and against my heart.

Back upstairs in bed, looking out again,
I see soft colors—
pink, yellow, purple and orange—
on the horizon.
Sea smoke rolls gently
over quiet waves.
The sun is rising now
on this,
the coldest winter morning.

Tjaakje C. Heidema

Towards Dusk

When I visit my sister in the park,
each day towards dusk
we get in the car
and ride around
hoping to see a moose.

Many times we have spotted
the dark brown neck of the aloof,
independent elk, the soft
buckskin and velvet
antlers of the elusive
deer, an eagle, a bear.

But we always look
for the one whose movements are fettered
by its intent on routine,
who stands alone
in quiet waters
near the edge
of the night
leaving a picture of peace
in the mind
for the soothing dream.

We must have seen
this once or twice
to know it so well,
or was it our father
we watched
stand so all alone
at dusk
in a field close to home?

A Damp Towel

Stepping out
of my shower,
I see
your blue, still-damp towel
hanging on the ivory-colored bar.

Quietly, slowly,
I pull the latch on the door
—just to make sure—
and with tired sighs
stand with your towel
wrapped around me,
smelling your smell,
feeling your wetness
against my thighs.

Then, hoping not to leave a trace,
I fold it perfectly
and hang it
back in place.

Tjaakje C. Heidema

Barter with your Shoes

Barter with your shoes
or bake a bread
to beat the blues.
They are gifts for you
for just a song
to enjoy
and to pass along.

There's enough to share
for all of us;
we can live a gentle way
with little fuss.
Let all your props
just fade and disappear;
there actually isn't much to fear.

Competing with your friends
and always striving to be best
is as defeating
as disliking your own breasts.
Dying and being left
is sad,
but living when you've killed
feels so very bad.

Love,
laugh,
play,
and run,
just, please,
don't buy a gun.

Fall In the Midst of Summer

The leaves and stalks of a budding plant
towards the bottom
in the shade—under the bushy part—
have turned orange, yellow and brown.
What a bummer!

I tear and cut away at the colors
wanting everything to be
green and alive
all at once.

The desperation in my efforts
takes my breath away
and tightens my chest.

I sit back exhausted
and cannot help but wonder.
Why is it so hard to accept
the colors of fall
in the midst of summer?

CPSIA information can be obtained at www.ICGtesting.com
265097BV00001B/4/P